ISBN 978-1-331-83245-4
PIBN 10239605

1 MONTH OF
FREE
READING

at

www.ForgottenBooks.com

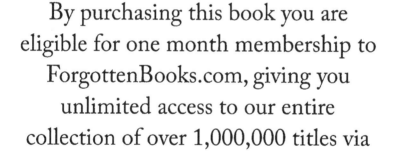

By purchasing this book you are eligible for one month membership to ForgottenBooks.com, giving you unlimited access to our entire collection of over 1,000,000 titles via our web site and mobile apps.

To claim your free month visit:
www.forgottenbooks.com/free239605

English
Français
Deutsche
Italiano
Español
Português

www.forgottenbooks.com

Mythology Photography **Fiction**
Fishing Christianity **Art** Cooking
Essays Buddhism Freemasonry
Medicine **Biology** Music **Ancient
Egypt** Evolution Carpentry Physics
Dance Geology **Mathematics** Fitness
Shakespeare **Folklore** Yoga Marketing
Confidence Immortality Biographies
Poetry **Psychology** Witchcraft
Electronics Chemistry History **Law**
Accounting **Philosophy** Anthropology
Alchemy Drama Quantum Mechanics
Atheism Sexual Health **Ancient History**
Entrepreneurship Languages Sport
Paleontology Needlework Islam
Metaphysics Investment Archaeology
Parenting Statistics Criminology
Motivational

VALIANT FOR THE TRUTH;

OR SOME MEMORIALS OF

GEORGE FOX AND THE EARLY FRIENDS.

BY

RUTH S. MURRAY.

"We are nothing; Christ is all."
G. Fox.

CAMBRIDGE:
Printed at the Riverside Press.
1880.

The Riverside Press, Cambridge:
Printed by H. O Houghton and Company

To

TO MY HONORED FATHER,

This Volume

CONTENTS.

CHAPTER I.

1624–1649.

CHAPTER II.

1650–1652.

CHAPTER III.

1652–1654.

CHAPTER IV.

1654–1656.

CHAPTER V.

1656.

CHAPTER VI.

1657–1659.

CHAPTER VIII.

1660–1661.

CHAPTER IX.

1663–1664.

CHAPTER X.

1663–1666.

CHAPTER XIII.

1673–1677.

CHAPTER XVII.

1689–1690.

INTRODUCTION.

I⊤ seems especially fitting that a brief yet trust-
worthy narrative of the life and religious services of
that eminent apostle of spiritual christianity, George
Fox, should be published at this time.

Nor will it detract from the interest or usefulness
of the publication, that his biography involves an
outline history of that great awakening of the English
nation, through the Lord's blessing on his instrumen-
tality, about two centuries ago, which resulted in the
gathering of the Society of Friends, and their establishment as a living and working church of the Lord
Jesus Christ.

So many questions have arisen, moreover, of latter
time, in regard to the faith and doctrines of these
our forefathers, that it is well that such a narrative
involves, of necessity, a clear and authentic exposition
of the blessed truths of the gospel as they were assuredly believed in and proclaimed by George Fox
and his followers with unwavering fidelity.

A careful reader of the political history of Great
Britain during the seventeenth century, and of the
civil and religious commotions which followed each
change in the ruling dynasty, will not wonder very
much at the error into which some have been led in

this regard, by a superficial review of the controversial writings of the early Friends. They lived, indeed, in troublous times; and it would seem, at the first glance, as though their whole life-work had been an aggressive and defensive warfare against principalities and powers in church and state.

Yet before they entered on this warfare these true soldiers of the cross had taken care to put on the whole armor of God, and so were thoroughly equipped for the conflict.

They knew their heads to be covered, as with a helmet, in the day of battle, with the assured hope of salvation through a crucified and risen Lord and Saviour: His righteousness was to them an unfailing breastplate, and their loins were girt about with His eternal truth. With the shield of an experimental faith in Him, they were able to quench all the fiery darts of the wicked one; and they wielded, in the name of the Captain of their salvation, the Sword of the Spirit, which is the Word of God, — often realizing it to be quick and powerful, and mighty through God to the pulling down of strongholds — even that Word which by the gospel is preached unto us.

Any one who will faithfully read the contemporary narrative of their lives and labors in that gospel, as well as their voluminous doctrinal writings, will see that they were sound in the faith of Christ, and filled with His love even to their enemies; and that their primary object was the salvation of their fellow-men, and the advancement of the kingdom of their Lord and Redeemer upon the earth.

He will plainly see, too, that the warfare they were

involved in arose for the most part from the determined opposition of His enemies ; or through the wiles of His great enemy, Satan, in blinding the eyes of many of the Lord's dear children, so that they should ignorantly oppose and persecute His own faithful servants.

We do not claim for these grand old reformers that they themselves were infallible in all their judgments of men and things ; nor in all their expositions of Divine Truth and interpretations of the divine oracles.

Building, as they were obliged for the most part to do, the walls of their Zion, like the Lord's people of old, with one hand, while they held in the other a drawn sword, ready for the conflict, we would not affirm that even these wise master-builders never in their haste made use of untempered mortar ; that the sound of the hammer or axe or any tool of iron was never heard in their building ; or that every stone was always smoothed and squared and fitly joined together in their spiritual temple.

Yet we may affirm that they both knew and testified that " other foundation can no man lay than that is laid, which is Jesus Christ ; " and that upon this Rock they sought to build His church, not with " wood, hay, or stubble," which a day of fire would consume, but bringing their most costly offerings, as it were, their " gold, silver, and precious stones, " in loving consecration to their Saviour's feet, and counting nothing too near or too dear to part with for His sake.

It was an age of general excitement and controversy upon religious subjects. Ecclesiastical domination and tyranny, first of one ruling sect and then of another, kept both pen and tongue in constant exercise with those who sought to establish, or defend, their liberty of religious belief or practice.

Yet while all non-conformists felt the pressure of the times, it fell most heavily on George Fox and his immediate followers, who believed themselves called to establish and defend a singular profession of faith, equally obnoxious to all the other prevailing sects, but which they claimed to be founded on the authority of the Lord Himself, opening up to them the Holy Scriptures in their true spiritual significance.

As we look now over the whole field of acrimonious controversy, in the calm light and with the cool judgment of history, we may well regret that these armed warriors, on both sides, had not oftener, before the conflict, drawn aside their visors ; and so, beholding the seal of the Lamb on each of their foreheads, have been enabled to recognize one another as beloved followers of the same Lord and Master whom they were equally desirous to serve, and whose truth they were both seeking zealously to defend.

It is a joyful thought, however, that they know each other now, and that many of them have clasped hands on the other side of the river. We willingly forget the opprobrious epithets mutually hurled at one another, in remembering that Bunyan, with the host of christian pilgrims which he has been the chosen instrument of leading to the " celestial city," and Baxter, with the multitude whom his " Call to the Unconverted " had awakened, or his thoughts on the " Saint's Rest " had comforted, are now lovingly mingling in ceaseless songs of praise, with George Fox and the early Friends, in that innumerable company which surround the throne, all having come out of great tribulation, and having washed their robes and made them white in the blood of the Lamb.

The doctrine which awakened the most general opposition throughout the professing christian church of that day, — and which George Fox and his followers considered it their especial mission to proclaim, — was what they termed " *the light of Christ;* " affirming that, by the grace of God, this light was given to every man, enabling him to see his own sinful condition, and by obedience to its manifestations to realize his soul's everlasting salvation, through faith in the Lord Jesus Christ, his Saviour.

This doctrine was continually misrepresented by their contemporaries, — and a fearful heresy and schism in the Society of Friends, in the last generation, was but the result of that continued misrepresentation, — as teaching that this light was a *principle within*, which, as they watched its gradual growth, would enable men to pass from a state of nature to a state of grace.

The difference between the two doctrines is all the difference between truth and error, between the delusions of a mystical spiritualism, on the one hand, and the fulness and simplicity of the gospel of Christ, on the other.

George Fox, from the earliest period of his public ministrations, as a young evangelist, to the date of the last epistles from his trembling pen, held the same unmistakable language, taught the same unchangeable truth.

6

"I showed them," he says in his Journal, under date 1651, "the true worship, which Christ had set up, and distinguished Christ, the true Way, from all the false ways; opening the parables to them, and turning them from darkness to the true Light; that by it they might see themselves, their sin, and Christ their Saviour, and believing in Him, they might be saved from their sins."

Again :—

1655.

"From Worcester we went to Tewksbury, where in the evening we had a great meeting. I turned the people to the Divine Light, which Christ, the Heavenly, spiritual Man, enlighteneth them withal; that with that Light they might see their sins, and that they were in death and darkness, and without God in the world; and might also see Christ, from whom it cometh, their Saviour and Redeemer; who shed His blood and died for them; who is the Way to God, the Truth, and the Life."

Turning now over nearly five hundred pages of his Journal, embracing a wondrous record of the faithful services and sufferings of this eminent servant of the Lord for more than a quarter of a century, we find in one of his epistles the same clear theology declared which he had at first preached :—

1678.

"Therefore I warn and advise you, both high and low, priests and people, to come to the Grace, Light, and Truth that comes by Jesus Christ; and also to come to the manifestation of the Spirit of God that is given to you to profit withal — that *with this Grace,*

Truth, Light, and Spirit of Christ, you may turn to Christ Jesus ᵞfrom whence it comes, who saith, Learn of Me ; and God saith, This is my beloved Son, hear ye Him. . . . .

" And therefore every one must believe in the light, if they *do receive Christ Jesus ; and as many as receive Him,* He gives them power to *become the sons of God.*

" So he that *hath the Son of God hath life,* and he that *hath not the Son of God hath not life."*

Ten years later, under date Sixth Month, 1687, he testifies that it was by this light, — " by this Holy Spirit the holy and righteous God doth drăw people from their unrighteousness and unholiness to *Christ ;* the righteous and holy One. . . . . And they *that mind the drawings* of the good Spirit of the Father *to the Son,* they do know that *Christ is their Mediator* and *makes their peace with God ;* and they do know that Christ is their High Priest, made higher than the heavens, *and hath died for their sins and doth cleanse them with His blood* and is *risen for their justification, and is able to the uttermost* to save all that come to God *by Him."*

In his epistles to the Friends in America, he exhorted them " to instruct and teach the Indians and negroes, and all others, *that Christ, by the grace of God, tasted death for every man, and gave Himself a ransom for all men, to be testified in due time ; and is the propitiation for the sins of the whole world."*

It was the Lord Jesus Himself, whom George Fox preached and exalted in his ministry, as the Light, the Life, the Door, the Way, the Shepherd, the Lamb slain from the foundation of the world, — the great Head and High Priest of His church, which He had bought with His own precious blood.

He believed, moreover, not only in the atoning efficacy of the blood of Christ, for the sinner's redemption, but also in its perpetual cleansing power, in the life of the forgiven, redeemed child of God ; and that by its complete operation on the soul of man a state of constant acceptance and purity, in the Light of the Lord, might be realized. He thus replied to some unscriptural teachers of that day : —

" *Of what value, price, and worth have they made the blood of Christ, that cleanseth from sin and death*, and yet told people that they would bring them to a knowledge of the Son of God, and now tell them they must not be perfect on the earth, but carry a body of sin about them to the grave. . . . .

" *But I say, you are redeemed by Christ. It cost Him His blood to purchase man out of this state he is in in the fall*, and bring him up to the state man was in before he fell."

" *So Christ became a curse, to bring man out of the curse ; and bore the wrath, to bring man to the peace of God ;* that he might come to the blessed state, and to Adam's state which he was in before he fell ; and not only thither, but to a state, in Christ, that shall never fall. And this is my testimony to you and to all the people on the earth." — *Epistles.*

Enough has been said to show the sound evangelical theology of George Fox. His personal character was beyond reproach ; even his enemies testified of him that " he was stiff as a tree and as clear as a bell and

that nothing could move him." The touching and
wonderful testimonies recorded by many of his friends
who knew him intimately, and loved and honored him
as few earthly leaders were ever loved and honored,
are still preserved, bound up in his writings.

We learn from them how graceful he was in countenance, how manly in person, and grave in gesture,
how courteous in his demeanor toward all; how in-
fluential in moving other men's spirits, while " very
much master of his own," how a civility was his
above all forms of breeding. We see him, while
" valiant in asserting the truth, bold in defending it,
patient in suffering for it, immovable as a rock " in
refusing to compromise it, yet forgiving and loving
to all his own persecutors and enemies.

He died, as he had lived, true to his Lord and
Saviour to the end. The last epistle he wrote, a few
days before his death, closes with these solemn words:
" So all of you live and walk in Christ Jesus ; that
nothing may be between you and God, but Christ in
whom you have salvation, life, rest, and peace with
God." And now, as was testified of him nearly two
centuries ago, this faithful servant has entered into
the everlasting rest and joy of his Lord, and there we
leave him, earnestly praying that we, in our day and
generation, may discharge our duty as faithfully as
he did his, and may not fail to preserve with loving
care the sacred trust committed to us also, to keep
and to hand down to future generations unimpaired,
— the evangelical spiritual doctrines of the gospel of
our Lord and Saviour Jesus Christ.

THOMAS KIMBER.

1*

CHAPTER I.

THE county of Leicestershire in the centre of England is one of the richest in agricultural resources. The land gently sloping to the River Soar, that passes through its midst, is covered with rich verdure, and affords nourishment to the cattle for which the county is famous. The bright waters of the river rippling gently over the smooth pebbles and shining sands, the bunches of alder and hawthorn bursting into flower in the early spring, and the velvety turf with the sheep and oxen grazing upon it, form a beautiful picture of quiet country life. But every landscape has its shadow, and a part of Leicestershire is very flat and marshy, reminding one that toil and labor belong to this stage of existence; that to-day, as of old, is sounded the declaration, "In the sweat of thy face shalt thou eat bread." It was amid hardship and poverty that the hero of this sketch passed his early days. In a humble weaver's cot in the village of Fenny Dayton, lived Christopher Fox, an honest, upright man, called by his neighbors "Righteous Christer." Here he plied his trade, patiently throwing his shuttle day by day, and receiving little for his toil. According to historians, even good workmen could earn only seven pounds a year.

"Righteous Christer's" wife, Mary Lago by name, came of martyr stock, and partook of the earnest steadfastness manifested by her ancestors, and we may imagine that her children were early trained in the love of truth.

Among the hearty, wholesome lads and lasses of the family, dressed in homespun clothes and living on barley and oatmeal, was one named George. Even in his childhood, differing from the others by his quiet, grave demeanor, his mother watched over him with tender care, endeavoring to cherish his good impressions and to strengthen his good resolutions. When very young he refused to join in the rude, foolish sports of the time, and when he saw old men engage in them the thought rose, as he tells us, in his childish heart, " If ever I come to be a man, surely I shall not do so."

When eleven years old, he says, " I was taught how to walk to be kept pure. The Lord taught me to be faithful in all things, and to act faithfully two ways, namely, inwardly to God and outwardly to men, and to keep to yea and nay in all things ; that my words were to be few and savory, seasoned with grace ; and that I might not eat and drink to make myself wanton, but for health." " The child is father to the man," and this conviction of the honesty, moderation, and temperance enjoined upon christians increased and deepened with his riper years.

Such an earnest, truth-loving boy was considered fit for the priest's office by his mother and some of his relations ; but others objecting, he was apprenticed to a grazier and had the care of his cattle. The shepherd boy found many opportunities for thought, as he sat watching the flocks feeding in the meadows, and his seriousness and gravity increased, while his truthfulness and steadfastness were such that the neighbors said, " If George says Verily, there is no altering him."

The foolish boys in the village might laugh at him for his soberness, but George, with all his quietness, was as bold as a lion in defense of right, and cared not for their ridicule.

One day, when he was nineteen years old, he was obliged to go to a fair on business. In that time, fair day was a season of great importance to all the villagers, old and young. There the sober farmers bartered horses, sheep, and oxen, while tempting wares of all kinds were displayed in the booths arranged round the green. Here the mothers gossiped and bought their supplies, while the youths and maidens made it a time of revelry, and the children, lost in admiration at the wonderful things before them, bought lollipops and candy with their cherished pennies. Well was it if the tempting ale and beer did not affect some of those present to such a degree that quarrels and broken heads were the results of " going to the fair."

Here George met one of his cousins from another town, who asked him to drink a jug of beer with him and some of his friends. They were all professors of religion, and George, who always sought such company, being thirsty, went into the booth with them. After taking one glass they called for more, and began to be very noisy, drinking the health of the king, and behaving in a rude, boisterous manner. George was shocked with such conduct, and pulling a groat from his pocket threw it down on the table to pay for his beer, and left them. He finished his business and went home, but could not sleep that night. His heart was distressed at the wickedness around him, and he prayed and cried to God for help. In his distress he seemed to hear the language addressed to him : " Thou seest how young people go altogether into vanity, and old people into the earth ; thou must forsake all, both young and old, and keep out of all, and be a stranger to all."

" Then," he says, " at the command of God, on the ninth day of the seventh month, 1643, I left my relations, and broke off all familiarity or fellowship with old and young." For four years he traveled from one place to another, seeking rest. His distress of mind was very great, and Satan at times tempted him to despair of ever receiving mercy through Christ Jesus. He received much attention from religious professors, but could find none to give him the help he needed. Protestant England was at that time divided into three sects, — Episcopalians, Presbyterians, and Independents. Great profession of religious faith and strict attention to outward forms of religion marked the time, but a lack of vitality in christian life was evinced in all the sects. There were among them all persons of sincere piety who were living devoted lives, while it must be confessed some put on the garb of religion merely to cover sinister designs. This was, as has been said, an age of polemic strife, and opinions were promulgated and maintained with much asperity. The disputants often lacked the loving spirit of Him whom they wished to serve, and bitter and severe persecution was the consequence of difference of sentiment from the dominant party, in church as well as state matters.

George Fox, in his trouble, found very little outward help. He says, "I went to many a priest to look for comfort, but found no comfort from them." The priest at Drayton, his native town, loved to argue with him, for he found George so well versed in the Scriptures that he could obtain from him material to use in his sermons to his flock.

Another to whom he went, in Manchester, told him to chew tobacco and sing psalms. But George says, " Tobacco was a thing I did not like, and I was in no state to sing ; I could not sing." Again, one advised he should be bled and take physic ; but this could not heal the malady of his soul. And the poor young man was in so much trouble that, to use his own words, " I longed in the daytime for the night, and in the night longed for the day, so heavy were my sorrows upon me." Many and earnest were his endeavors to find peace. He studied the Bible till he almost knew it by heart ; he spent days and nights alone in the woods ; he practiced long fasting, and gave money to the poor ; but all was unavailing.

Failing to find comfort from the priests, he tried the Dissenting ministers ; but in them his hopes were disappointed, and at last he saw there was no man could speak to his condition. But the Lord, whom he had been blindly seeking in the teachings of men and by his own works of righteousness, was not unmindful of His child. His promise is, " Seek and ye shall find ; " and now that George renounced all outward help, he heard a voice saying, "There is one, even Christ Jesus, can speak to thy condition, and when I heard it my heart did leap for joy." Now his bark, which had so long been tossed about, was anchored in the sure haven of his Saviour's love, and he says, "I saw that there was an ocean of darkness and death, but an infinite ocean of light and love which flowed over the ocean of death, and in that I saw the infinite love of God." And so sure was he of his deliverance that he adds, "I had been brought through the very ocean of darkness and death, and through and over the power of Satan, by the eternal, glorious power of Christ." Thus, like the Psalmist, he realized being brought up out of " the horrible pit and miry clay," and, with his feet on the rock Christ Jesus, he was able to sing the praises of Him who called him "out of darkness into his marvelous light." Longing that others should also know of this great salvation, he asked the Lord what He would have him do, and felt that he must go into the world and proclaim the blessed truths that had been revealed to him. Like Paul, he conferred not with flesh and blood, but, at the age of twenty-two, commenced the evangelistic mission which only closed with his life, and in which, through suffering and grievous imprisonments, he patiently and steadfastly performed his Master's bidding.

Before pursuing the life of George Fox, let us take a glance at the customs of the age, as described by historians. The court of James I. was distinguished by extravagance in dress and revelry. It seemed, when that monarch was transferred from the scantily furnished palace of Holyrood to his luxurious quarters in England, that his desire for dress and personal ornament became a perfect frenzy. His courtiers followed in his train, and at the accession of Charles I. the same passion continued. Wearing his hair in long, flowing curls, his dress sparkling with jewels, and redolent with perfume, the Cavalier looked with disdain on the closely cropped hair and sober dress of his Puritan neighbor, and laughingly called him Roundhead. These two names afterwards became the rallying cry on many a bloody battlefield.

While the men thus spent their time and money in the adornment of their persons, the process of dressing a court lady was said to be "as complex and tedious as the fitting out of a man-of-war." The wife of a nobleman of Charles's court, presenting a list of her wants to her husband, declares she will be satisfied with an allowance of £6,000 a year for her own personal requirements, with £10,000 more for jewelry.

This was not the only evil of the day. Such profuse expenditure required liberal means, and gambling, both among men and women, was resorted to as a favorite pursuit. Bribery was also extensively practiced. There was hardly a crime committed which the judge could not be induced to pardon, by the application of liberal bribes. Usurers and pawnbrokers increased to an alarming extent; and many ancient estates were lost to their owners by their extravagant living.

Strong lines of demarkation separated the different classes in society. The nobility looked down on the merchant, and he·in his turn disdained the artisan. The mode of addressing them was different. Only a great merchant was worthy to prefix Master or Mr. to his name, and the addition of Esquire would have thrown the court into a tumult. The judge must be termed Most Worshipful, the minister Reverend, and the whole style of conversation was full of unmeaning compliments. Among the country people and mechanics, the pronouns thee and thou were always used, but it was considered a great insult to address a person of higher rank in this manner. He was supposed to embody in his person a consequence equal to two or more ordinary individuals.

By a proclamation of James I., games, sports, and shows were allowed on the Sabbath, provided they did not interfere with the times appointed for divine worship. These were carried to such excess that the effect of the teaching of the morning seemed almost lost by the demoralizing effects of the folly of the afternoon. Many earnest people were distressed at these offenses, and longed for the opening of a better day.

Into this ground, so overrun with error, George Fox felt called to thrust the plowshare of truth ; and having the presence of the Master, he fearlessly set forth on his mission. His aim was to teach the iusufficiency of a mere assent to the truths of the Scriptures and of an outward acknowledgment of the redemption of our Saviour, without a personal appropriation of them.

He proclaimed the necessity of the new birth, the

transformation wrought in the heart, by being baptized into Christ, which would enable the believer to walk in newness of life, and the constant feeding of the soul upon its Lord, without which no christian life can be maintained.

Thus men settled upon the rock and foundation, Christ Jesus, who made peace between God and them, would be in a condition to be guided by His Spirit, which would lead them into all truth. Leaving their idle, frivolous lives, they would be enabled to live as becoming God's children. Speaking the truth in love, they would avoid unmeaning compliments, would use the same language to rich and poor, and, not being anxious to receive honor one from another, would seek the honor that cometh from God only.

He declared that all wars and fightings were utterly at variance with the teaching of our Saviour, and that therefore His servants could not fight. Remembering the injunction, "Swear not at all," he taught that all oaths were improper for a Christian; that men ought to lead such honest lives that their simple word would be sufficient. The truths of the gospel being freely given to man by his God, George Fox maintained they should be delivered with equal freedom and without payment; that men and women were one in Christ, and consequently both were included among His disciples, and were called to witness for Him in the world and engage in the ministry of the gospel. Uncovering the head and bowing the knee, he taught, were acts of worship to God, and should be reserved for Him alone. This might seem a small thing to us, but it occasioned great rage among the judges and magistrates of that day, who bitterly persecuted George Fox and his friends for their seeming lack of reverence.

Believing too much time and expense were involved in the clothing of the body, he dwelt on the necessity of simplicity in dress and in the style of living, though he never taught uniformity. Desirous of avoiding even the appearance of evil, he discarded the names of the months and days, which had been given in honor of pagan deities, and substituted numerical names for them.

These new and startling truths attracted much attention. Many who had been longing for a better way eagerly listened to the announcement that He who died for them at Calvary, to redeem them from the guilt of sin, was their ever-living Saviour to keep them from its power. The weary ones who longed for guidance joyfully embraced the truth of the abiding presence of His Spirit in their hearts, and thus a company was gradually gathered who separated themselves from the existing modes of worship and held meetings by themselves. They gave themselves the title of the Friends of Truth, but the people called them the Children of the Light, from their frequent use of Paul's advice to " walk as children of the light."

The onward progress of this sect and that of their bold undaunted leader will be related in the following pages.

CHAPTER II.

THE years during which George Fox had been engaged in such mental struggles were years of great excitement in the political world in England. A frightful civil war had been going on; King Charles had been forced to fly from London, and finally, taken prisoner by his own subjects, found he had only left his prison-house to die in front of his palace of Whitehall on the 27th of First Month, 1649.

With the monarchy in ruins, the Independents in Cromwell's army fierce in their onslaught upon all worship of images, the power of the bishops and clergy of the Episcopalians lost for a season, the quiet gatherings of the Friends continued to increase, and the declaration was often made, "The Lord *is* with them."

Early in 1649 we find our young evangelist going to a meeting of Friends, at Nottingham, on First Day morning. Seeing the great steeple-house, as he called it, he felt the Lord sent him there with a message. He said nothing to any one, but, leaving the Friends quietly sitting in their meeting, went to the place. The minister took for his text the words of Peter: "We have also a more sure word of prophecy," which he told the people was the Scriptures. George Fox says: "I could not hold in, but was made to cry out, 'Oh no, it is not the Scriptures,' and I told them what it was, namely, the Holy Spirit, by which holy men of God gave forth the Scriptures." It must not be imagined George Fox desired to undervalue the Holy Scriptures by these words. It would be difficult to find a more earnest Biblical student, or one who more frequently recommended their perusal. He carried a Bible about with him, which he frequently used when preaching, and was always ready to prove his doctrines by a reference to Scripture truths. And from their earliest rise the Society of Friends has always accepted and regarded the Bible as the outward rule of faith and practice, by which the truth of the teaching of the Holy Spirit in the heart is to be proved. But there was great need in that day of turning the thoughts of the people to Christ Jesus the Heavenly Teacher, who by His Spirit could open their understandings to comprehend Scripture teachings, that its precious truths might be savingly known, and hence this interruption.

It must also be remembered that this was a day of great religious discussion and also of great liberty. It was by no means an uncommon occurrence for some in the meeting to dispute or confirm the teachings of the minister after he had finished speaking. This instance is the only one mentioned in which George Fox interrupted the speaker, for in all his future attendance at churches he either waited till invited to speak, or till the service was over.

At this interruption, the officers, who seemed to be always on hand, took him away and put him in a close·dirty prison, where he was kept till night, when he was brought before the mayor, aldermen, and sheriff. They asked why he had disturbed the meeting, and he told them he had been moved of the Lord to do so. He was sent back to prison, but the head sheriff was so impressed by his words that he sent for him to come to his home. As George Fox entered the door, the wife of the sheriff met him and said, "Salvation is come to our house." The influence of his teachings extended over the whole family, and he afterwards held great meetings in Nottingham. Such a change was wrought in the husband and father that, remembering he had wronged a woman with whom he had traded, he sent for her, acknowledged the wrong, and made restitution. The next market-day he said to George Fox, " I must go into the market-place and preach repentance to the people," which he accordingly did.

The magistrates, feeling afraid of George Fox's influence, took him from the house of the friendly sheriff and sent him back to prison. But he had won warm friends in Nottingham, and at the next assizes, or session of the court, one of them came and offered to be bound for him, or even to give his life, if the young preacher could be released. George Fox makes this simple record in his journal, " The Lord's power is very great." After a time he was released from prison, and left Nottingham with a fame of the power of his ministry attending him which caused many to come to him for help, even from bodily infirmity.

He soon, however, had occasion to prove the truth that the disciple is not above his Master. Being one day in a meeting-house at Mansfield-Woodhouse, he attempted to speak to the minister and people, but they fell upon him in great rage, beating him with their Bibles, and everything they could lay hands on. Nearly smothered and sadly bruised, he was finally pulled out of the crowd and set in the stocks for some time. He was at last brought before the magistrate, who, seeing his pitiful condition, set him at liberty; but the people were so bitter against him that they followed him out of the town, throwing stones at him. Scarcely able to move, he contrived to reach a house about a mile distant, where he was kindly received and cared for, and says, " The Lord's power soon healed me again." Even on this stormy occasion he rejoiced, for " some people were convinced of the Lord's truth, and turned to His teachings."

But now he was to learn that

" They also serve, who only stand and wait,"

for the next year of his life was spent in the jail at Derby. He attended a lecture in the city of Derby, on the 30th of Tenth Month, 1650, and, after the services were over, spoke to the company assembled. They quietly listened, but after he had finished, an officer told him he must come before the magistrates.

For eight hours they were questioning him about his doctrines, apparently unable to decide what to do with him. He says, " They asked me if I had no sin." " Christ my Saviour has taken away my sin, and in Him is no sin," was the reply. " How we knew that Christ did abide in us?" " By His Spirit which He has given us." They temptingly asked if any of us was Christ. I answered, " Nay, we

are nothing, Christ is all."" Weary with examining
him, they finally committed him and one other who
was with him to the House of Correction for six
months.

The hopelessness of being delivered from sin in this
life was the theme of professors of religion then, as it
often is now, and the magistrates of Derby, failing to
apprehend the only source of strength, the power of
a living and ever-present Saviour manifested in the
nothingness of man, considered him as blaspheming
instead of glorifying Christ.

Though in his prison opportunities for preaching
Christ were circumscribed, he could write for his
Master, and many missives went out to the justices,
priests, and mayors, warning them against oppress-
ing the poor, or imposing false oaths.

The keeper of the prison was at first greatly incensed against him, but one day came to him trembling, as the jailer came to Paul and Silas, saying he
had been plagued, and his house had been plagued for
his sake. He remained all night with his prisoner, and
unburdened his heart to him, confessing that he had
done wrong in restraining George Fox from preaching, for his words were true. Next morning he went
to the justices and told them his house was plagued
for the sake of this innocent prisoner, to which one of
them replied that the plagues were on them, too, for
keeping him. This was Justice Bennet, who was the
first to give the name of Quaker to this sect, because
George Fox bade them tremble at the word of the
Lord.

Anxious to be delivered from their troublesome

2

prisoner, they gave him leave to walk a mile every day, hoping he would walk away. Secure in his innocency, George Fox would not help them out of their dilemma, and bade them measure a mile for him that he might keep within bounds.

Like Paul and Silas, he could sing praises even in his dungeon, and in a letter to " Friends and other tender people," we find these expressions : " O you who know the light, walk in the light. For there is peace in resting in the Lord Jesus. For the Lord who created all and gives life and strength to all is over all and merciful to all. So to Thee be all the glory. In Thee is my strength, my refreshment and life, my joy and my gladness, my rejoicing and glorying forevermore."

A soldier in Derby, desiring knowledge of the true way, came to him, and George was enabled to preach Jesus with such power that the soldier went away declaring his colonel was " blind, to cast the servant of the Lord into prison." This enraged the colonel, and the next year at the Worcester fight he endeavored to put the man in an exposed position. However, the soldier escaped unharmed, and his time of service having expired, being convinced of the evil of war, he left the army.

The youth, as George Fox was often called, is next placed in rather an anomalous situation. When the time of his commitment had nearly expired a call was made for more soldiers. Those who had been stationed at the north had frequently heard George Fox, and were desirous of having him for their captain. He was accordingly brought before the commissioners and soldiers in the market-place, and offered the position. He declined, saying he lived in that life and power that took away all occasion for wars. Thinking he but complimented them, they renewed their offer with many flattering words. Our sturdy friend was not to be overcome in that way, and positively declined. This excited their rage, and the jailer was commissioned to take him to the dungeon for rogues and felons. Here in a dirty, close place, with thirty felons, he was kept for another six months, his only liberty being a walk in the garden at times. Many thought he would never live to come out, but he felt there was more service for him to perform, and quietly waited the Lord's time.

He was not so much occupied with his own privations as to forget others, and wrote earnestly to the judges and magistrates on the subject of the punishment of death for trifling offenses, and the great harm ensuing from the practice of keeping prisoners so long in jail, where they learned wickedness one of another. One young woman was imprisoned for stealing money from her master. On her trial George Fox tried to influence both judge and jury to mercy, but without effect. She was condemned and led out to execution, but at the last moment was reprieved. She was brought back to prison, and soon afterward, repenting the errors of her past life, became a Christian.

The uneasiness of the magistrates increased at having so wrongly imprisoned George Fox, but they could not tell what to do with him. Like the apostles of old, he would not leave his prison until they had set him free ; and at last, in the beginning of the winter of 1651, they turned him out of the jail, and sent him on his way.

Traveling on as before in the work of the Lord, he came to Balby and Wakefield, where James Naylor, Richard Farnsworth, William Dewsbury, and others were convinced of the truth, and became his fellow-laborers. We shall meet some of these again in future years.

Pursuing his way through Yorkshire, preaching as he went, we hear of him in different places: at one time in the great minster at York, where the people threw him down the steps and trampled upon him; again, holding meetings in large houses that were freely offered, because he felt it his duty to show that the steeple-house was not the only place where God would meet with His people: then, on a haycock, with a crowd around him anxious to hear him, he sat in silence for some hours, to show that words alone would not bring a blessing; again, amid a company of Ranters, directing them to the inward Teacher, Christ Jesus their Saviour; and everywhere, the Lord was with His servant, and some ministers and justices, as well as many of the common people, were convinced of the truth he proclaimed.

One night he reached Patrington, and warned the people to repent and turn to the Lord. Here his faith was tested, for on seeking lodging at an inn none would receive him, neither would any one sell him anything to eat. He went out of the town, took a little water from a ditch, and sat under a furze bush till the break of day. As he started in the morning on his journey, a man with a pike staff went along with him three miles to the next town, where he called out the constables, and roused the people before sunrise. Nothing daunted, the youthful evangelist preached the everlasting truth to them all, and exhorted them to repent. They seized him and took him back to Patrington, a crowd of noisy men with pikes, staves, and halberds guarding this one unarmed man, who had eaten nothing the day previous and was weary with the night's exposure. While the minister and people were counseling what to do with him, a kind-hearted man called him into his house and gave him some bread and milk; after which he was taken nine miles farther on to a justice, who, on examining him, said he was no vagrant, and set him at liberty. He went back again to Patrington, and declared the truth, and this time many received his message, and a meeting was soon established there.

He was urged by the friendly justices whom he had met to make complaint of any who molested him; but he says, " I was not at liberty to tell anything of that kind, but was to forgive all."

In pursuit of his evangelistic mission he traveled through the year 1652, calling at the houses of great men, exhorting them to repent, sometimes lovingly received, sometimes slighted; sitting under a haystack one night, weary and footsore with traveling, and the next kindly sheltered by those who loved the truth. But as he himself says, " Good report or bad report was nothing to me, the one did not lift me up nor the other cast me down. Praised be the Lord."

He was now frequently joined by those who had been convinced by his teachings in some of his earlier visits, whose sympathy and assistance comforted him greatly. Passing into the West Riding of Yorkshire, though there was much opposition to him, he found many among the learned and powerful who were obliged to confess that they believed his principles must go over the whole world. George Fox himself says, " The Lord told me, if but one man or woman were raised up by His power to stand and live in the same spirit that the apostles and prophets were in, that one would shake the country for ten miles round." Hence his earnestness in calling the people to follow the dictates of that inward Teacher, the sure and unerring Guide of all the Lord's humble children.

Many foolish stories were circulated about him, that he rode on a great black horse, and would be seen in one county upon it in one hour and at the same time in another county sixty miles off, and that he carried bottles of which he made every one drink that followed him, thus bewitching them. As he traveled on foot and had no horse, these stories gradually died out.

He was now in a mountainous, barren region where there were few roads, and where the inhabitants for many years had pursued the even tenor of their way little affected by the events in the other parts of the country. This district was destined to become a stronghold of Quakerism, the truth falling simply on the untutored residents, who were untrammeled by educational or conventional forms.

Coming to a great hill, Pendle Hill, he ascended to the top with difficulty, and saw the extensive prospect before him. Not with the eye of an artist did he scan the scenery, but with the rejoicing of a christian warrior, he says, " The Lord let me see in what places He had a great people to be gathered." " A great people in white raiment, by a river side, coming to the Lord," was a comforting vision to him, and into the fields white unto harvest he joyfully thrust his sickle.

Gathering some fern and bracken for a bed, his first night was spent on an open common, and he then went on to the vicinity of Sedburgh, where he had seen the great company coming to the Lord. Here he found many who, dissatisfied with the established religion, had withdrawn from public worship. These gladly received his teachings, and a large meeting of Friends was established there.

A great fair to be held in Sedburgh, drawing together the population of a district of three hundred miles, afforded an opportunity not to be missed. Going up and down in the motley crowd he declared the day of the Lord, and, exciting much attention, was urged to go into the large church near by to preach to the people, but refused. Two large yew-trees grew in the church-yard, under which, seventy years before, one of the earlier Puritan ministers had preached, after he had been turned out of his church for non-conformity. Under these venerable trees, mounted on a bench, another non-conformist now stood, preaching for hours the word of life. Some said he was mad, and some received the truth with joy and became his helpers in the gospel.

In a dreary region about five miles distant, where nothing was to be seen but barren moorlands, and scarcely a human habitation, stood a small Episcopal chapel. Adjoining this building was a large rock, with a spring of water at its foot. Refreshing himself at the spring, this earnest laborer mounted the rock, and for three hours preached to the thousand people who had followed him into this desert place. To many that day the desert blossomed as the rose, as they eagerly embraced the glorious truths of the gospel, proclaimed by one who could testify that Christ Jesus was all in all to those who would receive him. Several of the most remarkable ministers among the early Friends came from this neighborhood: Francis Howgill, Edward Burrough, George Whitfield, and others, who faithfully served their Master, even unto death.

CHAPTER III.

THE winter of 1652 opens a new era in the life of our young champion for truth, and the scene changes from a bed of ferns and bracken, with the starry beavens for his canopy, to a stately hall in Lancashire, the ancestral home of Thomas Fell, a noted barrister of Cromwell's court.

Having risen rapidly to place and power, Judge Fell at last became dissatisfied with the administration of government, and returned to the practice of his profession and to his home at Swarthmore Hall. This commodious house was built in the Elizabethan style, with a spacious hall, rich oak panelings, and oriel windows. Possessing ample means, both Thomas Fell and his wife loved hospitality, and the doors of their home were open to all, especially to the ministers of the gospel. Margaret Fell was a descendant of Anne Askew, who laid down her life for the sake of her religion in the reign of Henry the Eighth. She evinced the same desire to know the truth that had marked her martyr ancestor, but thus far had not found rest. She says of herself, " I was seeking and inquiring about twenty years."

George Fox came to Ulverstone in his journeyings, and as Swarthmore Hall was only a mile distant one of his friends brought him there to spend the night. Judge Fell was absent in Wales, but he was courte-

2*

ously received by the lady of the house who had heard
of this singular reformer of Fenny Drayton, and desired much to see one of whom so many contradictory
reports were in circulation. The minister of Ulverstone, William Lampits, was there also, and in the
conversation which ensued Margaret Fell was obliged
to confess that the views advanced by George Fox
were true.

Next day was Fast Day, and she asked her guest to
go to church with them, but received the reply, " I
must do as I am ordered by the Lord." While walking in the fields he felt it was right to join them, and
going into the meeting-house found the congregation
singing. As the close of the hymn he stepped forward, mounted a bench, and asked permission to speak
to the assembly. This was granted, and he spoke
with much power on the necessity of a spiritual life,
" that he is not a Jew who is one outwardly, but he
is a Jew who is one inwardly, whose praise is not of
men, but of God." Margaret Fell had never heard
such teaching, and rising up in her pew, she leaned
forward fearing to lose a word.

Justice Sawry called out, " Take him away." But
a gentle, firm voice came from the judge's pew, querying if this stranger had not as much right to speak
in this place as others to whom permission had been
granted. This settled the point; and the preacher
went on explaining the Scriptures to them, directing
them to Christ, the Light of the world ; till Margaret
Fell, bursting into tears, cried out in her heart, " We
are all thieves, we have taken the Scriptures in words,
and known nothing of them in ourselves."

They returned to the Hall, and many of the servants were convinced of the truth of the new doctrine.
Their mistress, however, was under a cloud. Her husband was from home; she knew not how he would
like this new teaching, and yet in her inmost soul she
saw it was the truth, and could not deny it. But
courage was given her as to Annie Askew of old, and
embracing the truth in the love of it, she cast her
burden on the Lord, and calmly waited her husband's
return.

Great was the surprise of Judge Fell to hear, as he
came near his home two weeks afterwards, that a
great disaster had befallen his family; that there were
witches there, and if he did not send them away the
country would be undone. Such was the story told
him by Justice Sawry and others, who crossed the
sands of Levan on purpose to meet him and prejudice his mind against these new teachers. The judge
came home greatly offended with his wife, who had
heretofore proved worthy of his trust and confidence.

James Naylor and Richard Farnsworth were at the
Hall, and entered into conversation with him, in which
they displayed so much wisdom and condescension
that the anger of the judge cooled down. George
Fox came that evening, and had a long conversation
with them, showing that Christ was the teacher of
His people and their Saviour. The judge was satisfied there was no danger from the witchcraft against
which he had been warned, and next morning, when
the minister Lampits came, he could make no impression on the mind of his former patron.

On the contrary, when the question was raised as

to where the new converts should meet to worship God, the judge offered them a room in his house. The great dining-hall, which had so often resounded with the revelry and mirth of banqueting parties, was now converted into a place of worship, and was used for that purpose till the year 1690, when a meeting-house was built near Swarthmore, by order of George Fox, and at his expense. So thoroughly had the whole family embraced the new opinions, that the next First Day Judge Fell and his clerk and groom were the only attenders on the ministry of Priest Lampits.

The doctrines embraced by Margaret Fell and those who gathered together in the dining-hall at Swarthmore may be expressed in her own words. Speaking of the light of Christ, she says: " As we waited in it, and dwelt in it, we came to witness a washing and cleansing by the blood of Jesus. Then we became very zealous for God and for His truth, and for the preservation of His people in the truth. Our hearts became tender, and we had pity for all people's souls that remained in darkness."

The idea of the immediate teaching of the Holy Spirit, and the stand taken by George Fox against the institution of a human priesthood and its tithes, excited great opposition among the clergy, many of whom had embraced the office for the sake of its emoluments, and failed to manifest the fruits of the Spirit of God in their lives. Those in Lancashire were aroused by this bold reformer, who so fearlessly uttered the truths of the gospel, though they were unable to answer his assertions.

At one time, meeting a company of ministers at

Swarthmore Hall, George Fox asked whether any of them could say he had the word of the Lord to go and speak to such or such a people. None dared say he had; and Thomas Taylor, an old man, confessed before Judge Fell that he never heard the voice of God sending him to any people. This confirmed Judge Fell in his persuasion that these ministers were wrong; and he finally gave up the attendance on their preaching, though he never joined the Friends. Thomas Taylor, convinced of his error, came to Jesus like a little child, and, receiving pardon and acceptance, straightway began to preach Him in sincerity. The next day after this interview, George Fox says of him, " The Lord opened Thomas Taylor's mouth so that he declared amongst them how he had been before he was convinced, and showed how the priests were out of the way." He joined Friends, refused any longer to receive pay for preaching, and during the remainder of his life, though suffering much opposition, faithfully served the Lord Jesus.

The anger and rage of the ministers were aroused by this secession from their ranks, and the evident growth of the despised Quakers. They excited the people to cruelty, and at many meetings George Fox and his fellow-laborers were beaten, stoned, and otherwise maltreated. But notwithstanding a prophecy, that within half a year they would all be put down, Sewell tells us that " it fared with those people as with trees which grow best when most lopped."

> " As by the lopping axe, the sturdy oak
> Improves her shade, and thrives beneath the stroke,
> Tho' present cross and wounds severe she feel,
> She draws fresh vigor from the invading steel."

Judge Fell urged George Fox to make complaint against his persecutors, but he refused to do so, preferring to leave the matter to the Lord, and thankfully makes this entry in his Journal: "The Lord's blessed power which is over all carried me over this exercise, gave dominion over His enemies and enabled me to go on in His glorious work and service for His great name's sake. For though the beast makes war upon the saints, yet the Lamb has got and will get the victory."

The early part of the year 1653 witnessed great changes in England. Oliver Cromwell, desirous of the supreme power, was gradually bringing matters to that issue; and perceiving a disposition on the part of some in the Parliament to prevent this, summarily dismissed them after a sitting of thirteen years. Differing from the Protector, who was endeavoring to advance his own purposes, George Fox, as a single-hearted servant of the Lord, was laboring earnestly for the spread of the Redeemer's kingdom, unmindful of himself.

In Carlisle a stir was created by his coming, and the people thronged into the church in such numbers that George Fox could scarcely find entrance. There he spoke for three hours. "I declared to them," he says, "that every one that cometh into the world, was enlightened by Christ the Life, by which light they might see their sins, and Christ who was come to save them from their sins, and died for them; and if they come to walk in this light they might see Christ to be the author of their faith and the finisher thereof; their Shepherd to feed them, their Priest to

teach them, their great Prophet to open divine mysteries to them and to be always present with them."
Many, he tells us, were convinced that day, and received the Lord Jesus Christ and His free salvation.

From the Abbey, with its attentive crowd of listeners, he went to the castle, where the soldiers, assembled by the beat of the drum, received his message gladly. At the market-cross he preached that the day of the Lord was coming, that men should put away all cheating, and speak the truth one to another. The magistrates and their wives were very bitter, and sent the sergeants to arrest him, but the crowd around was so great they could not reach him.

The next First Day, however, after speaking in the church with so much power that the people shook and trembled, the mob assembled and began to throw stones at him. The governor sent some soldiers to bring him out safely ; but the next day a warrant was issued for his apprehension. Hearing of this, George Fox went to the hall, and had much conversation with the magistrates. There were many false statements made against him, and he was finally committed to prison, as a blasphemer, a heretic, and a seducer.

When brought thither the jailer manifested much civility at first, thinking to receive money from George Fox for his extra comforts. On finding he had nothing to expect, his behavior changed. George Fox was put in a room with no bed, and three soldiers were stationed to watch him. He was allowed no privacy ; and his enemies, the ministers, incensed against him because he taught the freeness of the gospel, came at all times to revile and abuse him. So general was the idea that he was to be hung that many, even ladies of rank, came from curiosity to see the man who was to die. The judge and sheriffs dared not bring him to trial, owing to some error in the indictment, but left him to the malice of his enemies.

He was finally put down in the dungeon among a wicked crew of thieves and murderers, under a very cruel jailer, who often beat him with a great cudgel. "While he struck me, I was made to sing in the Lord's power ; then he fetched a fiddler and set him to play, thinking to vex me thereby," but George Fox with his singing drowned the noise of the fiddler, and made his persecutors go on their way.

Among those who came to see him was James Parnell, a boy of sixteen, who was so impressed by his teaching that he became a Friend, as the members of the new society began to be called. Discarded by his relatives, who had given him a liberal education, and persecuted for his religion, he bore it all with much patience. Not by long serving however, was he to honor his Lord, for in the nineteenth year of his age he was imprisoned in Colchester Castle, and suffered such hardships as caused his death.

He was put by the cruel jailer into a hole in the wall, called the oven, so high from the ground that he had to reach it by a ladder, which being six feet too short, he was obliged to pull himself up to the hole by a rope. His inhuman jailer refused to allow him to raise his food by a cord and basket ; and benumbed by the confined position in which he was obliged to sit, it was with much difficulty he could go up and down for his meals. One day, going up with his food in his hand, he caught at the rope, but missing it, fell down on the stones. He was so bruised and wounded by the fall that he died a short time after, a true martyr to his faith.

The Little Parliament summoned by Cromwell, consisting mostly of members of his own choice, heard that at Carlisle a young man was imprisoned who was to die for his religion. The Parliament caused a letter to be sent down, inquiring into it. Two of the justices who were friendly to George Fox also wrote a letter to the magistrates, condemning their course, and the prisoner, from his dungeon, sent out a stirring appeal to all who denounced him to come forth and make good their accusations against him. The governor soon after came to the prison, and finding such a noisome place, censured the magistrates for allowing this treatment, and put the under jailer, who had been so cruel, into the same prison. Soon after this those who imprisoned George Fox, being somewhat afraid of the consequence of their actions, set him at liberty and he resumed his labors.

The enemies of the reviled Quakers, finding their predictions false as to their extinction, now began to prophesy they would soon become poor and chargeable to their respective parishes. This failed also, for their character for honesty and uprightness was such that the first inquiry in any place was for a tradesman who was a Quaker. The cry now was altered, and they said: " If we let these Quakers alone they will take the trade of the nation out of our hands." George Fox thus records his prayer for the new converts : " My desire is that the Lord God may be glorified in their practicing truth, holiness, godliness, and righteousness amongst the people in their lives and conversation."

Many meetings being established in the north of England, a large band of workers was now ready to go southward and carry the good tidings. About sixty went, two by two, east and west as the Lord directed, and their loving friend, younger than some in years but older in the truth, felt constrained to write to them an epistle of advice and counsel : " This is the word of the Lord God to you all. Friends, everywhere scattered abroad, know the power of God in one another, and in that rejoice. Believing in the light, you shall not abide in darkness, but shall have the light of life ; and come every one to witness the light that shines in your hearts, which will give you the light of the knowledge of the glory of God, in the face of Jesus Christ. And keep your meetings every - where, being guided by God, that you may see the Lord God among you."

Among his relatives in Lancashire he had many conflicts. Nathaniel Stevens, the minister at Drayton, sent for him to come there, having engaged several other ministers to be present at the discussion. Knowing nothing of their schemes George Fox went, and was enabled by the Lord to silence all their disputations. His father, though a hearer and follower of Stephens, was so pleased with his son, that he struck his cane into the ground and said : " Truly I see, he that will but stand to the truth, it will carry him out."

There being rumors of a plot against Cromwell, the soldiers were ordered to apprehend all doubtful characters, and at one of the meetings George Fox was arrested. Colonel Hacker, the leader of the band, told him he might go home if he would hold no more meetings ; but he said he was an innocent man, and free from plots ; if he should promise, it would manifest he was guilty of something, ending with the declaration, he should go to meeting if the Lord ordered him. " Well then," said Colonel Hacker, " I will send you to my Lord Protector by Captain Drury." Arrangements were accordingly made to send him to London ; but before leaving, George Fox asked for an interview with Colonel Hacker, and kneeling by his bedside besought the Lord to forgive him, telling the colonel, when his day of misery and trial was come upon him, to remember what he had said to him.

Afterwards, when Colonel Hacker was in prison in London, and under sentence of death as one of the judges who condemned Charles I., he told Margaret Fell he remembered what he had done against the innocent, and was troubled by it.

CHAPTER IV.

THE London which George Fox entered in 1654 would scarcely be recognized by a resident of the present city. It was surrounded by walls whose foundations were laid by the Romans, and could only be entered through embattled gateways. Within these walls was a labyrinth of narrow lanes, of which Cheapside and Cornhill were the most conspicuous. The upper stories of the houses overhung the lower, so that acquaintances could shake hands from the opposite windows, while the street below was like a covered way. There was no provision for lighting the streets at night, and the different classes in society jealously maintained the distinction of rank. The courtiers had an exclusive right to lanterns, merchants and lawyers were accompanied by boys with links, while mechanics and other artisans must be content with torches. The busy, bustling Strand was the connecting link between London and Westminster, then a distinct city, and instead of being crowded with stores, as at the present day, was lined on either side from Temple Bar to Charing Cross with the houses and gardens of bishops and noblemen.

During Cromwell's Protectorate religion was the prominent topic of the day. Knotty points of doctrine were discussed with as much zest as the state of the markets is now. Outdoor preaching was very common, and crowds would stand patiently three or four hours at a time to listen to eminent preachers. Of one of these, named Howe, it is recorded, that on a fast day he preached for seven hours, with a recess at noon for refreshment. Notwithstanding the length of the sermons, these meetings were not very helpful, and there was a strong desire among many to see some of those Quakers who had arisen in the north of England, and of whom so much was said.

Isabel Butten came to London early in the year 1654, and found two brothers willing to open their houses for all who wished to assemble to worship in this new way. These were the first meetings of Friends held in London. Isabel was busy one First Day evening in St. Paul's Church-yard, circulating some papers written by George Fox, when she was arrested for Sabbath breaking and carried before the Lord Mayor. He committed her and her compauions to Bridewell, among the abandoned and guilty, thus showing the fanatical spirit of the times.

Among the sixty ministers, mentioned in a former chapter as going out from the north on their Master's service, were two, very different in age and character, but who were united in their zeal for the truth. These were Francis Howgill and Edward Burrough. Both came from Yorkshire, and their simple appearance and provincial dialect did not make much impression at first upon the subtle Londoners. Their wisdom and zeal, however, produced great effect; and, borne up by a strength not their own, the fruits of their ministry increased to such an extent that after three months of service many other meetings were established, besides the two in the houses of the brothers Dring, and room could hardly be found for the numbers who assembled.

At last a large meeting-place, known as the Bull and Mouth, which would hold one thousand, was obtained. Here, amid wrangling and contention, some extolling the Quakers and some accusing them of heresy, Edward Burrough, the younger of the two evangelists, would take his stand on a bench, with a Bible in his hand, and speak to the tumultuous assembly before him, with so much power that all became calm and attentive.

At one time a large company of rude journeymen and apprentices was gathered together at Moorfields to witness a wrestling match. The victor, who had overcome many, was walking about the ring, challenging others to fight him. Edward Burrough, stepping up to him, spoke a few words in a calm, quiet manner. Then, turning to the spectators, he called upon them to fight the good fight of faith, whose prize was not the wrestler's honor but a crown of life immortal. The sport ceased, and at the end of the sermon the crowd dispersed. More than one acknowledged afterwards that their first impressions of good had been received that day.

Both F. Howgill and E. Burrough laid down their lives for their religion, — the former in Appleby Jail, where he was imprisoned for life; Edward Burrough in Newgate. After ten years of successful ministry this young Boanerges, as he was called, was shut up with a hundred others in such close quarters that many died of jail fever ; one of these was this zealous evangelist, at the age of twenty-eight.

But to return to George Fox. Coming as a prisoner to London, his caretaker evidently trusted his honor, for he was lodged at the Mermaid near Charing Cross while Captain Drury went to inform the Protector of his arrival. Oliver Cromwell had not as much fear of this dangerous prisoner as his soldiers evinced, for he simply required that George Fox should write a promise to abstain from taking up weapons against the Protector or his government. Owning no Master but Christ, George Fox wrote to the Protector what the Lord gave him to write, declaring that he was a man of peace, and was sent of God to witness against all violence, and to bring people from the causes of war and fighting into the peaceable gospel.

Feeling curious to see this strange man, Cromwell sent for him to come to Whitehall. The interview was different, somewhat, from the ordinary routine of court ceremonial, for George Fox went to the Protector with a sense of the responsibilities of his position, and exhorted him to "keep in the fear of God, that he might receive wisdom, and order all things under his hands to God's glory." Congenial as they were in some respects, further conversation brought the two nearer together, and at parting Oliver Cromwell took the hand of the sturdy reformer, saying : " Come again to my house, for if thou and I were but an hour or a day together, we should be nearer one to another." Cromwell ordered that Fox should be conducted to the great hall to dine with the gentlemen in waiting; but this honor was declined by the honest Quaker: "Tell the Protector," said he, "I will not eat of his bread or drink of his drink." When he heard this, Cromwell said: "Now I see there is a people risen and come up that I cannot win with gifts, honors, offices, or places; but all other sects and people I can."

Being set at liberty, George Fox went back to his inn, where many came to hold converse with him; some with good intent, others only to mock and revile; but the Lord was with His servant, enabling him to preach the gospel with power. He held meetings in London so large that he could hardly get to and from them for the crowds. So many joined the Friends that the Presbyterians, Baptists, and Independents were greatly disturbed. Even in the Protector's house and family were found some of the despised Quakers, and in a song of thanksgiving the disciple thus extols his Master's faithfulness: —

"The God of heaven carried me over all, and His blessed power went over all the nation, insomuch that many Friends about this time were moved to go up and down, to sound forth the gospel in most parts of England and also in Scotland, and the glory of the Lord was felt over all to His everlasting praise."

Not only with his tongue, but with his pen, did this zealous follower of the Lord call the world to the knowledge of the truth. To those who professed to be christians he writes cautioning against an outside show of religion, and exhorting to singleness of heart. His address "To such as follow the world's fashions," draws a vivid picture of a fine lady and gentleman of

the Commonwealth, with their dress vanities and pas-
times. These he admonishes to leave the devil's adorning and seek the ornament of a meek and quiet spirit,
which is, with the Lord, of great price.

The journeyings of the Friends were not confined to
England, but some were sent by the Lord to Holland
and Italy, even to Rome itself. The expenses of
their journeys of course were heavy, and as many of
those who embraced these principles were often imprisoned, their families required care and assistance.
Nobly did the early Friends fulfill their duty toward
their brethren, dispensing wisely, as good stewards,
the gifts bestowed upon them.

Gerad Croese, a Dutch historian, gives this character
of them : "They were merciful, liberal, and compas-
sionate to the miserable and afflicted in body or mind ;
every one helped, either with substance, counsel, or assistance, as his capacity allowed, and the necessity of
his neighbor required ; so that none wanted for anything." He also speaks of a worthy man, who hearing much of this singular people came to England on
purpose to see for himself, and found, like the Queen
of Sheba, the half had not been told him. He soon
joined the Society.

The oath of adjuration against King Charles came
out this year, and as Friends refuse all oaths, it was
used by the envious magistrates as a snare in which
to catch them. Many were imprisoned and suffered
cruel hardships for their faithfulness in refusing to
swear.

George Fox addressed a letter to the Protector,
warning him of the injustice of casting the followers

of Christ into prisons for obeying His commands. But Oliver Cromwell's heart was not as tender as in the days when the earnest appeal of G. Fox brought tears to his eyes, and he did nothing toward alleviating the sufferings of Friends.

Notwithstanding this, one of the early writers under date Fifth Month, 1655, says, " Most of our army are scattered, broken, and cast into prison. The work of the Lord goes on, nevertheless. We have five or six meetings of Friends every First Day, besides two great places for a threshing-floor. Many are coming in, many inquiring, and many are convinced daily. Glory and honor forever be to the Lord l "

The early Friends seem to have soon found the necessity for two meetings, one for those who had embraced their principles, and others more public for the crowds of restless, turbulent inquirers.

As early as 1652, George Fox, in one of his epistles, gives this advice : " And when there are any meetings in unbroken places, ye that go to minister to the world, take not the whole meeting of Friends, but let them keep together and wait in their own meeting place. And let three or four or six that are grown up and are strong in the truth, go to such unbroken places and thresh the heathenish nature."

Leaving the work in London to some of his fellow laborers, George Fox with Edward Pyott and William Salt traveled through the southern counties of England. On coming to Cornwall they encountered opposition, and at Market-Jew the magistrates sent constables to arrest them. The Friends naturally asked for their warrant, and as they could show none, refused to go with them. Edward Pyott afterward went to the mayor and aldermen, representing their unchristian conduct in thus attempting to stop the Lord's servants, and they withdrew their summons.

Here George Fox wrote a paper of christian counsel and advice to the seven parishes of the Land's End, calling them to Christ and warning them against despising His law. In their journey next day, one of the Friends handed a copy of this letter to a man who gave the paper to his master, Mayor Ceely of St. Ives. When the Friends reached that town they stopped at a blacksmith's to have one of the horses shod, and George Fox went down to the seashore for a walk. Great was his surprise, on his return, to find the town in a tumult, and that his companions had been taken before Mayor Ceely. No one interfered with him, but he would not leave his friends, and followed them. The obnoxious paper was drawn out, and he was asked if he would own it. He answered, Yes. The oath of abjuration was then tendered them, but they could not take it. George Fox handed the answer he already had given to the Protector, but this was refused, and they put under the care of a body of soldiers, to be taken either to Pendennis Castle or Launceston Jail.

On their way, like Paul of old, they sought opportunities for preaching the gospel, and at Falmouth found some earnest sober people, who seemed glad to converse with them. The captain of the soldiers was not very well disposed toward his prisoners, and George Fox was obliged to send for the constables to protect them against his insults. The constable reproved the captain and his band, who promised to be more civil. They started again on their journey, the prisoners sowing some seed at Falmouth, which afterwards bore fruit, a large meeting being established there.

Captain Fox, the governor of Pendennis Castle, being from home, the prisoners were conveyed directly to Lancaster Jail. The crimes for which they were charged in the warrant were that they pretended to be Quakers, had spread several papers tending to the disturbance of the public peace, had no pass for traveling up and down the country, and refused the oath of abjuration. The weakness of the charges shows the determination then existing to persecute all who acknowledged the truth of Quakerism.

Now commenced a long imprisonment in a place where there were no Friends, and where every means were used to render their condition intolerable. It was nine weeks to the assizes, and during this time many came to see the strange men who said thee and thou to every one, and would not take off their hats or bow the knee to any. Curiosity in some cases gave place to sincere esteem and respect, as the simple, earnest teachings of the gospel were proclaimed, and the truth they heard found a place in the hearts of the hearers.

At the assizes, many came from far and near to hear the trial of the Quakers, every available space in the court room was filled, and people thronged the doors and windows. It was with difficulty the prisoners could be brought in. As they entered George Fox said, " Peace be amongst you." But the keeping on of their hats produced anything but a peaceful feeling in Judge Glyn, the chief justice, who angrily commanded them to remove them. This they could not consistently do, and after some debate they were remanded to prison.

Our sturdy reformer asked the judge to show him when any magistrate, Jew or heathen, from Moses to Daniel, required men to remove their hats before them. Judge Glyn was not ready with an answer then, but soon afterwards sending for the prisoners, asked triumphantly : " Come, where had they hats from Moses to Daniel ? I have you fast now ! " Nothing daunted, George Fox quietly answered : " Thou mayst read in the third of Daniel, that the three children were cast into the fiery furnace by Nebudchadnezzar's command with their coats, their hose and their hats on." Defeated in his argument, the judge had recourse to the usual cry : " Take him away, jailer."

In the afternoon they were again called out, and while pushing their way through the crowd, they heard so much swearing that George Fox tried to circulate a paper he had written against this sin. The paper being passed around among the jury, the attention of the judge was called to it, and he asked George Fox if that seditious paper was his. This was the wished-for opportunity, and the prisoner replied if they would read it aloud he would tell. The judge was unwilling to consent, but it was finally read, and in a loud voice George Fox acknowledged it was his and showed how it agreed with the teachings of Christ. Notwithstanding their imprisonment for nine weeks, and the false and foolish charges brought against them, they were remanded to prison until the next assizes.

Perceiving their detention would be long, the Friends sent away their horses into the country, and refused any longer to pay their weekly allowance of seven shillings for the hire of their rooms. The jailer, a most abandoned character, who had twice been branded on the hand as a thief, shut them up in a foul dungeon, called Doomsdale, which was the common sewer of the prison. The mud was over their shoes, and there was no place where they could sit or lie down. In this dreary place they were refused even a little straw and a light, but some people from the town, whose feeling of pity was aroused, brought them a candle and a few handfuls of straw. They burnt this to purify the air, and the smoke ascending through the floor into the room above, occupied by the under jailer and some thieves, exasperated them greatly. They poured down upon them through the floor everything that they could find, and used most abusive language.

George Fox and his friends were kept for a long time in this place before the jailer would allow them to have it cleansed. Often they were left without food or water, but their sufferings were somewhat mitigated after a time, and their confinement, even in this gloomy dungeon, was of service to their ministry. Many came to the prison to see and hear for themselves about this new doctrine, and one of the chaplains of the Protector said they could not do George

Fox a greater service for the spreading of his principles in Cornwall than to imprison him there. In the
words of the undaunted sufferer himself : " The
Lord's light and truth broke forth, and many were
turned from darkness into light, and from Satan's
power to God."

The love existing among the early Friends was very
strong ; for while George Fox lay in this cheerless·
prison, one of them went to Oliver Cromwell and
offered to lie in Doomsdale in his stead. The Protector, struck by this act of friendship, looked around
on his followers with the question : " Which of you
would do as much for me if I were in the same condition ? "

The Protector thought he had not the legal right
to accept the offer, but sent Major-General Desbour-
rough to Cornwall with instructions to release them
if they would go home and preach no more. This
they could not promise and so were retained some
time longer, but after six months imprisonment they
were set at liberty on the 13th of Seventh Month,
1656.

The jailer who so cruelly treated them lost his
position the next year, and was committed to the
same filthy place, locked in irons, beaten, and bade
to remember his former cruel treatment of the
Quakers. Here he died, leaving his family in poverty and distress.

Released from their house of bondage, the Friends
went on their way rejoicing and visited some who had
been converted through their teaching. After a little
time spent in this way they returned to Launceston to

see the company of Friends who had been raised up during their imprisonment. George Fox gives this pleasant account of their condition: "The Lord's plants grew finely, and were established on Christ Jesus their rock and foundation."

CHAPTER V.

ABOUT the time when the doors of the dreary jail at Launceston were opened, and the prisoners released, other and more severe punishments were preparing in the New World, for those who professed this hated religion.

In the seventh month of the year 1656, two women Friends arrived in Boston, Massachusetts, from England. They were cruelly treated, and shut up in prison for five weeks. Nicholas Upsal, an old resident of Boston, and an earnest christian, was much distressed at the condition of these poor friendless women. No food being provided for them, he induced the jailer to supply them, by paying him five shillings a week. They were only released from jail to be sent back to England.

A month after, a ship-load of Friends arrived in Boston, and although no law then existed against the Quakers, they were considered too dangerous to be allowed their liberty, and after a short imprisonment, were sent back to England. Governor Endicott now made a law, prohibiting masters of vessels from bringing Quakers to the colony, and threatening imprisonment to any who should come.

Honest Nicholas Upsal was sorely troubled at this unrighteous law, as it seemed to him, and remonstrated with the rulers against such edicts, warning

3*

them to take heed, lest they be found fighting against God. The rulers resented such interference, and the old man was fined twenty pounds, and banished from the colony.

The neighboring colony of Rhode Island offered an asylum for all who suffered on account of their religion. Roger Williams, its founder, had been banished from Massachusetts for his liberal views, and in arranging the government of his new home, declared that " the doctrine of persecution for the cause of conscience, is most evidently and lamentably contrary to the doctrines of Jesus Christ."

Thither in the depth of winter Nicholas Upsal bent his steps, and was kindly sheltered on his journey by an Indian chief, through whose encampment he passed.

The Indian could not understand why this feeble, aged person should undertake this journey at such an inclement season. But when he understood the cause, he offered to share his wigwam with the stranger, saying, " What a God have the English, who deal so with one another about their God."

The dreaded heresy grew and increased notwithstanding all the efforts of the rulers of the Massachusetts colony to check it, and more stringent laws were enacted. A fine was imposed on all who should absent themselves from public worship. No one could offer any refreshment to one of the hated Quakers without being fined, and all who held their views were sentenced to be whipped, lose their ears, have their tongues bored with hot iron, and if these measures did not induce them to recant, they were to be banished from the colony. Even children did not escape. In some cases they were condemned to be sold as slaves at the Bermudas, in payment of the fines imposed on their parents. But no ship captain could be found, who was willing to carry out this unjust sentence, and it was not put in execution. One of our own poets has drawn a graphic picture of this cruel imposition, in the ballad of Cassandra Southwick.[1]

Thus in the New World, as in the mother-country, the rapid spread of the Quakers caused much fear and perplexity. About this time, however, the extravagant acts of some of the sect aroused a strong prejudice against them. The life of James Naylor shows how weak man is, and how spiritual pride can blind the eyes even of those who have once known a risen Saviour.

He was the son of a Yorkshire farmer, and was a soldier in the Parliamentary army for eight or nine years, leaving the service on account of ill health. He was living at Wakefield, when George Fox passed through the town, on one of his preaching tours, and was attracted by the truths he heard. He thought upon them when working in the fields, and one day while following the plow, he felt the Lord called him, to go and preach the gospel. Waiting day by day upon the Master, for strength and guidance, he became an eminent minister, and many were converted through his preaching. A party of extravagant admirers gathered around him, chiefly composed of women, who in their enthusiastic admiration bowed before him, kissed his feet, and styled him the Prophet of the Most High.

[1] J. G. Whittier.

He was soon afterwards imprisoned at Exeter, and received a visit from George Fox, whose clear judgment pierced the veil of error, and caused him solemnly to warn James Naylor of his danger. Darkness had, however, blinded the eyes of the infatuated man, and he could not be convinced of any wrong. On parting he would fain have kissed his teacher, but the honest evangelist refused the tokens of friendship from one who had turned away from the Lord.

Experiencing with Paul the perils of false brethren, George Fox sadly writes in his journal: "So after I had been warring with the world, there was now a wicked spirit risen up among Friends to war against."

When James Naylor was released from Exeter, as he journeyed to Bristol, the frenzy of his admirers reached its height. They formed a procession to attend him, and even strewed their scarfs and handkerchiefs in his path, shouting hosannas before him.

These outrageous proceedings excited much attention, and the actors of this strange drama were arrested. In this day they would have been considered suitable inmates for an insane asylum, but Quakerism was so obnoxious that any pretext for oppression was gladly seized. Parliament took up the matter, and, urged by the Presbyterian and Independent preachers, who wished to destroy the whole sect, condemned him to cruel and ignominious torture. He was to be set in the pillory for hours, whipped by the hangman through the streets of London and Bristol, his tongue was to be bored with a hot iron, and his forehead branded with the letter B.

After this he was to be imprisoned at Bridewell. He bore his punishment with great patience, and in his solitary imprisonment the scales fell from his eyes. "My heart is broken," he writes to his friends, "for the offense I have occasioned God's truth and people. I beseech you forgive me." He made a full recantation of his conduct, and after his release from prison, in a large meeting at Bristol, spoke so feelingly of his sin, and of God's mercy in restoring him, that there were few dry eyes among his audience. His friends lovingly received the penitent, and the Lord again enabled him to preach the gospel, but his constitution was so weakened by his sufferings that he died in 1660 at the age of forty-three. In the hour of death he said: "There is a spirit I feel, which delights to do no evil, nor to revenge any wrong. Its ground and spring are the mercy and forgiveness of God, its crown is meekness, its life is everlasting love."

Though the truth of an indwelling Christ was thus grievously abused, yet as the counterfeit proves the existence of a reality, so it is this same truth which enables the Lord's children to walk in newness of life, by accepting a personal, conscious, loving union with Christ their living and ever present Saviour.

Although as a body Friends had disowned James Naylor's conduct, the same Parliament that pronounced this cruel sentence upon him, enacted a bill against vagrants, so worded that it could be used against Friends. By this, every idle person or vagrant who had not a good and sufficient business for traveling such as the justices might approve, could be punished as a rogue.

This gave great power to the magistrates who were not kindly disposed towards Friends, and many were arrested and thrown into prison. George Fox went to London to petition Oliver Cromwell to interfere on their behalf, but the Protector was not as accessible now as he had been, and nothing could be gained from him.

But though persecuted the Friends were not forsaken, as will be seen by the following extract from a letter of Richard Hubberthorne : —

" Though the waters of strife are up in floods at present, yet sweetly doth the water of life flow, and pleasant streams are drunk by those who keep patient in the will of God, and life, power, and glory from the Father, are more manifest than ever."

The good seed watered with many tears, and springing up amid many trials, was tenderly watched over by the Lord, and George Fox says : " Many mouths were opened in our meetings, to declare the goodness of the Lord, and some who were young and tender in the truth, would sometimes utter a few words of thanksgiving and praise." Wisely and with fostering care did the earnest shepherd watch over the lambs of the flock. He advised the older Friends to be very tender and careful how they admonished these, even though they might sometimes say more than seemed warranted. None but the openly profane were to be reproved in meetings, but if any felt like giving advice to the younger ones, it was to be done after the gathering, " in the wisdom which is pure and gentle, and in that love which bears long, suffers long, and fulfills the law."

" Thus," he says, " ye will find the power of God to chain, bind, and limit, so that nothing will come forth, but what is in the power, in which will be your joy and refreshment."

A new and untried field now lay before our earnest seed sower, in which he proved the truth of the words, —

> " Sow though the rock repel thee
> In its cold and sterile pride,
> Some cleft there may be liven
> Where the little seed may hide.
> Fear not, for some will flourish,
> And though the tares abound,
> Like the willows by the waters,
> Will the scattered grain be found."

Three years previously the fame of the strange sect in the north of England had reached Wales, and John Ap John had been sent by the minister of his parish to inquire what it meant. The teachings of George Fox and his coadjutors entered his heart, and like the good seed grew and flourished. Now, when Wales was to be the field for missionary labor, John Ap John was ready as a brother beloved to go with George Fox, and, by his acquaintance with the Welsh language, aid him in his teaching.

As in former journeys, they met with different treatment, in some places finding a rude, noisy crowd who tried to molest them, and again reporting " glorious meetings and many turned to the Lord." At one place they found an earnest company who believed the Scriptures, but had no knowledge of the guidance of the Holy Spirit. To these George Fox was enabled to preach Christ as their Saviour and their

Guide, and many were comforted by his teaching. After the meeting a justice of the peace came to him saying, " You have this day given great satisfaction."

They held an open air meeting at Radnorshire, where the people gathered in such numbers that some one told George Fox the people " lie like a leaguer," meaning as closely as if investing a city. A great longing for the salvation of souls pressed on the spirit of the Lord's devoted servant, and after seeking strength from his Master, he preached Jesus to this vast concourse as their Saviour, Redeemer, and Mediator. Notwithstanding the crowd, the stillness was so great that all could hear without difficulty, though many were on horseback. Gathering up the sheaves with rejoicing, the gleaner makes this entry in his journal : " Many were turned to the Lord Jesus, and his free teaching that day."

They found poor accommodations and rough treatment, and the honest laborer records with indignation that the oats were stolen from their horses. " A wicked, thievish people, to rob the poor dumb animal of his food. I had rather they had robbed us."

Under these adverse circumstances the Lord was their shield and protected them. On one of their journeys they were overtaken by a man of rank and wealth, who continued with them for a time, intending as he afterwards told them, to arrest them at the next town for highwaymen. But George Fox, ever ready to sow seed by the way-side, spoke so powerfully to him that instead of putting them in prison he invited them to his house. Both his wife and himself desired Scripture proofs for the doctrines professed by these wandering evangelists. These George Fox delighted to give, and taking out his Bible, several hours were spent in converse, and they parted with feelings of mutual regard.

They ascended the rocky sides of Caeder Iris, and surveying the scene before him with prophetic vision, many different localities were pointed out by this modern seer, where there would be " a great people raised up to the Lord." The predictions were remembered by John Ap John, and though no meetings of Friends then existed in those places, it was not many years before in every case, the result was that " a brave people were gathered in the name of the Lord."

An attempt was made at Dolgelly by two ministers to prove that the light to which John the Baptist bore witness was a created natural light. " But I took the Bible," says George Fox, " and showed them that the natural lights which were made and created were the sun and moon and stars, but the true light that lighteth every one that cometh into the world is Christ the Word, by whom all things were made and created. I directed them to that which would give to every one the knowledge of Christ who died for them, that He might be their way to God, and make peace between God and them."

A crowd had gathered to listen to the discussion, and John Ap John repeated the teaching in Welsh. The people eagerly received the truth, and with uplifted hands praised God for sending his messengers among them.

Different treatment awaited them after leaving

Dolgelly. Having occasion to cross a large ferry, they found a rude company on the boat who prevented John Ap John from coming on board. Perceiving this, George Fox leaped back on the shore to await the next crossing. This detained them till two o'clock in the afternoon, after which they had a journey of forty miles, and only one groat between them. They traveled all night, and at five in the morning found a resting-place for themselves and their tired horses.

Having traveled through every county in Wales preaching the everlasting gospel, and being comforted by the willingness with which many received the truth, he now turned his steps towards England. He reached Liverpool at the time of a great fair, and wishing to hold a meeting took a novel method of announcing this desire. A Friend was stationed at the cross at the market square to proclaim that George Fox, a servant of the Lord, would have a meeting the next day at such a place, and if any feared the Lord they might come and hear him declare the word of life unto them. The call was responded to by a large number, and "many were established on the Rock Christ Jesus."

Arriving at the hospitable home of his friends, the Fells, he tarried with them for a season, rejoicing with them in the mercies of their covenant God, who had cared for him in his journeying, and had watched over the little flock at Swarthmore Hall.

CHAPTER VI

ANXIOUS to work while it was day, the indefatigable laborer remained but two weeks at Swarthmore and then started for Scotland, having, as he says, "Robert Widders with me, a thundering man against hypocrisy and deceit."

This was a new field, and one in which he encountered much opposition. The free salvation which he preached was especially disagreeable in that land which lay under the dark shadow of unconditional election and reprobation, upheld by the ministers. But as the travelers passed from place to place the record is of "blessed meetings in the name of Jesus," and many conversions.

At Garshore they had a large meeting and George Fox plainly showed from the Scriptures "that Christ was a propitiation for the sins of the whole world, that He died for all men, the godly for the ungodly; and He enlightens every man that cometh into the world, that through Him they all might believe." "Many other Scriptures," he says, "were opened concerning reprobation, and the eyes of the people were opened."

But the defection from their ranks caused dismay among the Scottish ministers, and George Fox says: "A great cry was among them that all would be spoiled, for they said I had spoiled all the honest men

and women in England already, so according to their
own account the worst were left to them." Upon this
they gathered great assemblies of priests together, and
drew up a number of curses to be read in their several
steeple houses that all the people might say " Amen "
to them.

The actors in this scene have all passed away, and
it is not best to dwell long upon it. Of all disputes
it is well known those on theological questions are the
most fierce and bitter, and allowance must be made
for the rudeness of that day and time. It is cause of
rejoicing that in our day the lines of demarkation between those who love the Lord Jesus are becoming
very faint, and christians are so earnest in fighting Satan they have little time for warring with each other.

Nothing daunted by the opposition he encountered,
George Fox pursued his way as his Master directed,
being joined by James Lancaster and Robert Parker.
Warrants were issued against him, but he said : " If
there were a cart-load of them I do not regard them,
for the Lord's power is over all."

At Johnstons, the governor ordered that the Friends
should be sent out of the town. Surrounded by a
company of soldiers, these unarmed men left the place.
James Lancaster was " moved of the Lord " to sing
His praises with a melodious sound, and George Fox
to preach the everlasting gospel.

This sight called many to the windows, so the
Friends had the opportunity they desired of preaching Christ. They journeyed a little longer in Scotland, and after " a glorious meeting " at Edinburgh,
they left the country with the feeling that " many

were turned to the Lord and many more would be, though there was need of patience."

It appears from letters of the early Friends that soon after the rise of the Society, meetings were instituted for the purpose of considering the condition of the members and extending care over them. As all were considered members who wished to be, a great variety were gathered together, among whom were many poor in this world's goods who needed assistance. In 1653 a monthly meeting was established in Cumberland " to look after the poor, and see that all walked according to the truth." Similar meetings were established in other places, and finally a general meeting was held at Shipton for the northern and southern counties, " when in the wisdom of God they did see all walked according to the glorious gospel of God, and that there was nothing wanting among them." The first was held at the house of John Crook, Fourth Month, 20th, 1658. At this meeting notice was taken of the missionary laborers, especially those beyond the sea, and a collection recommended for the aid of gospel missions.

The following minute was prepared at a similar meeting in 1660, and sent through the different counties : —

" DEAR FRIENDS AND BRETHREN, — We having certain information from some Friends of London, of the great work and service of the Lord beyond the seas, in several parts and regions, as Germany, America, and many other islands and places, as Florence, Mantua, Palatine, Tuscany, Italy, Rome, Turkey, Jerusalem, France, Geneva, Norway, Barbadoes, Bermuda, Antigua, Jamaica, Surinam, Newfoundland; through all which Friends have passed in the service of the Lord, and divers other countries, places, islands and nations, and among many nations of the Indians, in which they have had service for the Lord, and through great travails have published His name, and declared the everlasting gospel of peace unto them that have been afar off, that they might be brought nigh unto God."

" A collection is then recommended in every particular meeting to be sent as formerly to London for service and use aforesaid." [1]

George Fox could not be absent from such a meeting, where his clear head and sound judgment would be very useful; and after the Friends had mostly left for their homes, a company of soldiers came to arrest him. He was walking in the garden at the time, and heard them inquiring for him, but after a little conversation with John Crook, they left without seeing their would-be prisoner, who again went on his missionary tour, giving this testimony to the faithfulness of his covenant God: " The Lord's power accompanying me, and bearing me up in His service."

As has been stated, this was the age of controversy, and a Jesuit in the suite of the Spanish Ambassador challenged all the Quakers to a dispute at the house of the Earl of Newport. The reply was that some of their number would meet him. His courage began to fail, and he insisted that only twelve should

[1] *Letters of Early Friends.*

come. This number he reduced to six and finally to three. George Fox, fearing lest the opportunity should be lost, hastened to the house with two other Friends. A long debate ensued on the purity of the Romish church, and the doctrine of transubstantiation. The Jesuit could not defend himself or his cause, and though most of the audience were his friends, they were obliged to confess that his subtilty was confounded by the simplicity of the truth.

Clouds hung heavily at this time over the Friends both in England and Ireland. Many were lying in dungeons under the care of cruel jailers, while their families were suffering for food. George Fox wrote an earnest letter to Cromwell beseeching his aid, but without avail. He seemed to have lost the desire for religious liberty evinced in the early part of his Protectorate, and pretending to disbelieve the statement of the sufferings of Friends, paid no attention to them. His dark days had now commenced, for his favorite daughter Betty, the Lady Elizabeth Claypole, lay ill with a fatal disease. For a fortnight the unhappy father watched by her bedside, unable to attend to any public business. During her illness, George Fox hearing she was troubled in regard to her soul's salvation, wrote a loving, encouraging letter, bidding her "look away from sin and transgression, to that which would take them away and bring peace," which letter was a comfort to the sick lady. She died on the 6th day of Eighth Month, and her father seems never to have recovered her loss, his own illness commencing on the 20th of the same month. For a time it was not considered serious, and he was able to ride out.

Being in the park at Hampton Court one day, George Fox met him. He embraced the opportunity to lay the condition of the suffering Friends before Cromwell. The feelings of the Protector were touched, and he bade George Fox come to him the next day. But at the time appointed Oliver Cromwell was too ill to be seen, and they never met again. On the afternoon of the 30th of Eighth Month, 1658, during a dreadful hurricane, so fierce that trees were plucked up by the roots, and travelers feared to start on their journeys, the summons came, and he who had wielded the sovereign power in England, lay powerless in the grasp of the mighty conqueror Death.

On the 8th of the following month Judge Fell also passed away. He had been a firm friend to the new sect who had often assembled under his roof, and though never connected with them, he had in his capacity of judge frequently stood between them and persecution.

Richard Cromwell quietly assumed the position of Lord Protector of England, but had neither his father's talent nor his skill in moulding the minds of other men, and his administration lasted only a few months.

Friends now applied to him for the redress they had vainly sought to obtain from his father, and an address was prepared stating the cases of the nineteen hundred and sixty who had been imprisoned in the last six years, and the one hundred and forty-four now lying in prison. No notice was taken of this, and it was followed in about ten days, by another remarkable document worthy to be remembered : —

"FRIENDS, — Who are called a Parliament of these Nations, we, in love to our brethren that lie in prisons and Houses of Correction and dungeons, and many in fetters and irons, and have been cruelly beat by the gaolers, and many have been persecuted to death and have died in prison, and many be sick and weak in prison and on straw; so we in love to our brethren do offer up our bodies and selves to you, for to put us as lambs in the same dungeons, and Houses of Correction, and their straw and nasty holes and prisons, and do stand ready a sacrifice, for to go in their places in love to our brethren, that they may go forth and that they may not die in prison, for we are willing to lay down our lives for the brethren, and to take their sufferings upon us, which you would inflict on them."

"We, whose names are hereunto subscribed, are waiting in Westminster Hall an answer from you."

This document was signed by one hundred and sixty-four Friends, and shows their claim to be considered the disciples of the Lord Jesus, by this manifestation of love one to another. In the Parliament this document excited various feelings. One member voted they should be whipped home as vagrants, but the decision was finally given that the signers of this paper should forthwith return home to their respective habitations, apply themselves to their callings, and submit themselves to the laws of the nation.

Although this appeal apparently failed, yet in the month following, a committee was appointed to inquire into the causes of the imprisonment of so many,

4

and how they might be released. Colonel Rich, Henry Vane, and others were on this committee, and they would fain have freed all who were suffering for conscience' sake, but the Parliament did not agree to their report, and nothing was done for the relief of Friends.

George Fox, fearing lest some should be "discouraged because of the way," wrote an encouraging letter to send out among Friends, in which he exhorts them to "fear not," because as they keep in the patience, resting in the Lord Jesus Christ, "they will find all things to work together for good to them that love God."

The disturbances in the nation increased every day. Those in power were plotting and contriving for their own selfish interests. The army was divided into factions, the weaker adhering to Richard, and the stronger in favor of General Lambert, as the most suitable person for Protector. Richard removed one difficulty by quietly retiring to Hampton Court and resigning his position. Everything seemed to be tending toward the restoration of the Stuarts.

Amid these intestine commotions George Fox, anxious that Friends should maintain their character of followers of the Prince of Peace, wrote earnest letters of counsel to them, beseeching them "to dwell in the fear of the Lord" and to have nothing to do with wars and fightings. A fear of coming evil impressed his mind with regard to the city of London, and he sent a letter to those in authority warning them of the consequences of their wicked actions.

General Monk's soldiers seemed to have a particular dislike to Friends, and treated them shamefully, tearing their clothes from them, and pulling by the hair and kicking both men and women. This was represented to their general and he issued the following order : —

"St. James, 9th of March.

" I do require all officers and soldiers to forbear to disturb the peaceable meetings of the Quakers, they doing nothing prejudicial to the Parliament and Commonwealth of England.

(Signed)　　" GEORGE MONK."

A singular circumstance is related of a wicked man in Somersetshire, who wished to disturb Friends in their meetings. Dressing himself in a bear's skin, he seated himself in front of the Friend who was preaching, and rolled his tongue out of his mouth to make sport for his followers. Returning from the meeting he stopped at a bull-baiting, and carelessly going too near, the animal stuck his horn into the man's throat, pushing out his tongue, so that it hung in the same manner in which he had pushed it out in the meeting. Thus impaled on the bull's horn, he was whirled round in a fearful manner.

Starting again on a missionary tour, George Fox came into Cornwall at a stormy time when there were many shipwrecks at Land's End. He was greatly grieved to find that the love of gain had so destroyed all kindly feeling that no effort was made to save the lives from these wrecks, but only to obtain treasure from them. Even those in authority connived at the practice, and participated in the gain. He issued a manly appeal to the parish priests and magistrates, and concluded with a postscript addressed to his own people : —

" All dear Friends who fear the Lord, keep out of the ravenous world's spirit which leads to destroy, and is out of the wisdom of God. When ships are wrecked, do not run to destroy and make havoc of ship and goods, but save the men and their goods for them, and so deny yourselves, and do unto them as ye would that they should do unto you."

This remonstrance awakened the better feelings of the people, and Friends at least afterwards avoided this cruel method of gaining wealth.

Thus moulded in no narrow form we find this bold reformer fearless in opposing evil in every shape, yet tender and ready to sympathize with all suffering.

CHAPTER VII.

THE contending factions in England were now in a state of great tumult, and the loyalists were eager to embrace the opportunity to restore Charles Stuart to his father's throne. General Monk, a man whose principles were of that convenient kind which could be easily changed, had command of the army in Scotland, and was feared and courted by all parties. He had been a Royalist before he was a Parliamentarian, and found no difficulty now in using his power in effecting the restoration of the King.

He sent letters to Charles, who was at Cologne, watching for an opportunity to assert his claim to the throne, and the result of their correspondence was the famous declaration of Breda, which Charles sent to the House of Lords, with a duplicate to the House of Commons.

This document, dated April 14th, 1660, was full of fair promises, and one paragraph particularly interested Friends, of whom one hundred and forty-four were now lying in prison for conscience' sake : —

" And because the passion and uncharitableness of the times has produced different opinions in religion, by which men are engaged in parties and animosities against each other, which when they shall hereafter unite in freedom of conversation will be better understood, we do declare a liberty to tender consciences and that no man shall be disquieted or called in question for difference of opinion in matters of religion which do not disturb the peace of the kingdom, and that we shall be ready to consent to such an act of Parliament as upon mature deliberation shall be offered to us for the full granting of that indulgence."

The Royalist party predominating in the House of Lords, it was soon decided to invite Charles to ascend the throne of his father. The young man accordingly sailed from the Hague, and landed at Dover Fifth Month, 25th, 1660, with his two brothers, James Duke of York and Henry Duke of Gloucester. From thence he went to London, greeted on every side by the joyous acclamations of his subjects. Sober men and women knelt down and asked for blessings upon him, holding up their little ones to look at him, that they might tell their children and grandchildren of that glorious day. The city of London was stirred to its very depths at his coming. The bells poured out their joyous greeting, bonfires were lighted, and crowds of people clad in holiday garb thronged the streets. The old Puritan plainness was studiously avoided, the Cavalier wardrobes were brought out, the French gentlemen and ladies of the court appeared in bright colors, and all seemed like a gala day when " the king came to his ain again."

In the midst of all this excitement, Friends pursued the even tenor of their way, though they rejoiced that the restoration had been peaceably accomplished, and felt a hope of some respite from persecution.

Richard Hubberthorne, writing to his friends at Swarthmore, Fifth Month, 29th, 1660, says : " This day King Charles and his two brothers, James and Henry, came into the city. Charles is of a pretty sober countenance, but the great pride and vanity of those who brought him in is inexpressible. He is in danger to be led into those things to which he himself is not inclined."

George Fox was pursuing his labors in Derbyshire and Nottinghamshire, and came to Shipton, where was held a general meeting of men Friends out of many counties, concerning the affairs of the church, both in this nation and beyond the sea.

The liberality of Friends was so well known that at this gathering at Shipton, two hundred of the poor of the neighborhood came, expecting some assistance. They were not disappointed, for the Friends sent to the bakers for bread, and gave every one a loaf; for as George Fox said, " We were taught to do good to all, though especially to the household of faith."

Swarthmore now offered a quiet resting-place to the earnest laborer, and after leaving Shipton George Fox came there, expecting to remain some time. But shortly after his arrival he was arrested by Henry Porter, a justice who had been a major under Cromwell, and now wished to commend himself to King Charles, by his zeal in apprehending those who refused the oath of allegiance.

The superstitious people of Furness, regarding the prisoner with feelings of awe, kept him all night at the constable's house, and set a guard of fifteen or sixteen men to watch him, some of whom sat in the chimney for fear he should " go up."

He was hurried off in great haste next morning, on

a little horse with neither saddle nor bridle. The soldiers who formed his guard amused themselves by beating the horse and making him trot and gallop. This troubled the tender spirit of their prisoner, and he slipped off the horse, telling them "they should not abuse the beast." So great was the hatred toward this unoffending person, that one man knelt down in the road, and thanked God that he had been taken prisoner. Thus they went on fourteen miles to Lancaster, the soldiers rejoicing in what they considered a victory, and George Fox "singing praises to the Lord for his triumphing power over all."

He was brought before Justice Porter, who accused him of being an enemy to the king and a disturber of the peace of the nation. The prisoner naturally desired to see the order by which he had been apprehended. Justice Porter refused to show it him, and after some conversation committed George Fox to the Dark House, to be a close prisoner till released by either King or Parliament.

Lancaster jail was a dreary place, and the jailer exceedingly cruel. None of the Friends were allowed to visit George Fox, although others were admitted, who abused and reviled him. ·Though prison walls now confined his body, they could not bind his spirit, and the innocent sufferer still performed all the service for his Master that lay in his power, at times preaching through his barred windows to the crowds who gathered to hear, again writing papers and letters to encourage Friends in the right, and to the King and others in authority, " to exhort them to the exercise of mercy and forgiveness."

Meantime his friends outside were busy on his be-half, and Margaret Fell, feeling indignant that the sanctity of her home should be thus invaded, wrote the following spirited appeal to the magistrates :—

" I do inform the governors of this nation, that Henry Porter, Mayor of Lancaster, sent a warrant, with four constables, to my house, for which he had no authority or order. They searched my house and apprehended George Fox in it, who was not guilty of any breach of law, nor any offense against any in the nation. After they had taken him, and brought him before the said Henry Porter, bail was offered, what he would demand for his appearance to answer what could be laid to his charge, but he, contrary to law (if he had taken him lawfully), refused to accept of any bail, and put him in a close prison. After he was in prison, a copy of his mittimus was demanded, which ought not to be denied to any prisoner, so that he may see what is laid to his charge; but it was de-nied him ; a copy he could not have, they were only suffered to read it over. Everything that was there charged against him was utterly false ; he was not guilty of any one charge in it, as will be proved and manifested to the nation. Let the governors con-sider it. I am concerned in this thing, inasmuch as he was apprehended in my house, and if he be guilty I am too. So I desire to have this searched out.

" MARGARET FELL."

As George Fox had been committed for high treason, he could only be released by a special order
4*

from the King, and Margaret Fell determined to appeal to him in person. She accordingly went to London accompanied by Ann Curtis, the daughter of a Royalist who had been hanged at his own door for his sympathy with Charles I., and who hoped to have some influence with the King on this account. Justice Porter said he would go too, and "meet them in the gap." But when he arrived in London he found too many who remembered him as a zealous parliamentary man, and soon had enough of the court.

Margaret Fell and her friend were kindly received by the King, who promised to send for George Fox to come to London. A writ of habeas corpus was accordingly issued, but when served, a difficulty arose: the expense of sending a guard with him to London. The sheriff would fain have put this upon his innocent prisoner, but he refused to bear any part of it. At last the sheriff told him, if he would promise to appear before the judges in London, he might be released. This inconsistency shows the true nature of those who apprehended him. This so-called dangerous fellow was released for the time on his own word, and a copy of his own accusation given him to present to the judges. He traveled as he pleased, in company with some of his friends, holding meetings by the way, and reached London in about three weeks.

The day after his arrival, he presented himself and his accusation before the judges of the King's Bench, but as they were occupied with other business, they ordered the marshal to take charge of George Fox till the next day, and give him a room to himself. The marshal said the prisons were so full he had no place to put him. Judge Foster then asked George Fox if he would appear the next day at ten o'clock in Westminster Hall. "Yes, if the Lord gives me strength," was the reply. The judge turned to his associates and said, "If he says yes and promises, you may take his word," and this pestilent fellow was again released to go where he pleased.

Next day he appeared, according to his promise, and the charges against him were read. When he heard the accusation against himself and his friends, of embroiling the nation with blood, and raising a new war, George Fox protested his innocence. He shrewdly asked: "Do ye think if I and my friends had been such as this charge declares, that I would have brought it up against myself? Had I been such a man, I had need to have been guarded with a troop or two of horse. But the sheriff and magistrate of Lancaster thought fit to let me and my friends come up with it ourselves, nearly two hundred miles, without any guard at all, which they would not have done if they considered me to be such a man."

The judges were convinced that the charges against him were groundless, and Esquire Marsh, a gentleman of the King's bed-chamber, testifying that it was the King's pleasure he should be no longer detained, they referred the whole matter to the King, who sent an order for his release. Thus after an imprisonment of twenty weeks he was set at liberty, and the malice of his persecutors fully exposed. George Fox was urged to take advantage of the law against them for his false imprisonment, but remembering the injunction, " Avenge not yourselves," he left them to the Lord.

There was now a little respite from persecution, for King Charles, true to his declaration at Breda, commenced his reign with a desire of granting full liberty of conscience. Richard Hubberthorne had an interview with the King, and stated the views of Friends in such a calm, convincing manner, that Charles said none should suffer for their opinions as long as they lived peaceably, and seven hundred Friends who had been imprisoned for their religious principles were now set at liberty. An order was even drawn up to allow Quakers the free exercise of their worship, and only lacked the signature and seal of the King, when an unforeseen occurrence threw them into greater suffering than ever.

This was the mad outbreak of the Fifth Monarchy men, a sect which arose in the time of Cromwell, claiming that the Lord Jesus was speedily coming to set up his throne upon the earth. Sir Henry Vane was one of the leaders of this party, and as he was now in prison with the judges of Charles I., it was supposed this revolt was partly caused by the desire to set him free.

On the night of the 6th of First Month, 1661, a wine cooper by the name of Venner, whose reason was unbalanced, inflamed some fifty or sixty visionaries by vehement preaching, and these men rushed from his conventicle in London, proclaiming King Jesus. The quiet city was hushed in sleep, but in a few moments there was a great uproar. The train bands were called out, and the instigators of the tumult fled into the country for two days, concealing themselves in the woods. On the 9th they returned in the open day, in the fanatical belief that neither bullets nor sharp steel could hurt them, broke through the city gates, routed all the train bands they met, and put even the King's guard to the run. They were finally overcome and most of them taken prisoners; the rest fell with arms in their hands, shouting that Christ was coming presently to reign upon the earth.

Notwithstanding the insignificant character of this outbreak, a feeling of uncertainty fell over the nation. Many high in rank were known to belong to the Fifth Monarchy men, and the Earl of Clarendon, desirous of establishing a standing army, increased the fears of people by announcing the danger of a great insurrection.

All dissenters were looked upon with suspicion, and Friends, though innocent of participation in any plots, had to bear the brunt of the persecution which followed. Armed men broke up their meetings, and both men and women were dragged from their houses to prison. Even the sick were not exempt, but were rudely taken to jail, one man dying as soon as he arrived there.

The city and country prisons were filled with Friends, and Margaret Fell went again to the King, to remind him of his promise; and she gave him an account of the thousands who were now deprived of their liberty, for no crime but of obeying what they believed to be the dictates of their God.

George Fox also drew up a declaration of faith addressed to the King, in which he proved that Friends could not be implicated in any such conflicts. " The Spirit of Christ which leads us into all truth will never move us to fight and war against any man with outward weapons, neither for the kingdom of Christ, nor for the kingdoms of the world. And all wars and fightings with carnal weapons we deny, who have the sword of the Spirit, and all that wrong us we leave to the Lord."

The testimony to the unlawfulness of all war was ever maintained by the Friends, and it is interesting to note the ground of their objection. George Fox said " he could not be a soldier because the spirit of strife was slain in him, and having been brought into a love for all could not, he declared, fight against any. His views were the fruit of his conversion, the result of the unrestrained working of the Holy Spirit in his heart." Thus down through the long vista of the ages we hear the echo of the declaration of the early christians, " I am a christian, and therefore I cannot fight."

The clouds were now lifted a little by this declaration and the fact that several of the Fifth Monarchy men, who suffered the punishment of death, fully exonerated Friends from any connection with them. The King finally issued an order that Friends should be set at liberty without paying fees.

An important case was tried at the assize in Nottinghamshire in the early part of the year 1661 concerning the validity of the marriages of Friends. While disowning the power of man to join persons in this solemn covenant, Friends had been very careful that the proceedings in this matter should be conducted with great care. Various preliminary steps were deemed necessary, to prevent all concealment, and at last the parties, in a religious meeting, made the declaration before God and man, that they took each other to be man and wife. The judge, after hearing both sides of the question, declared that this was all that was necessary for a legal marriage, and the question was never afterwards raised.

CHAPTER VIII.

WE will now turn from the contemplation of the labors of these earnest men, to follow some equally earnest, self-denying women, who left their comfortable homes and went forth, as they believed, at their Master's bidding, to carry the knowledge of the glorious gospel of Christ to the ignorant and blinded followers of false gods.

In 1660 Mary Fisher started alone on a perilous journey to visit the Sultan of Turkey. In those days it required great exertion to traverse Europe ; but after pressing through many difficulties she arrived at Adrianople, where Sultan Mahmoud was then encamped with his army. A message from her informed him that an Englishwoman had come with something to declare to him from the great God. An audience was granted, and the next morning she was ushered into the presence of the Sultan, arrayed in his robes of state, and surrounded by his officers, also splendidly attired. Into this scene of pomp and splendor came the simple Quaker, like David of old before Goliath, with no weapon of her own, but in the name of the Lord of Hosts. The Sultan, through his interpreters, courteously asked her to declare her message, and listened attentively while she spoke.

A Friend in such an interview would surely dwell upon the principle of peace, so often brought forward by George Fox, and so constantly practiced by himself and his adherents. The weak follower of the Prince of Peace returned to her home in safety, after delivering her message; but Sultan Mahmoud, though seemingly at the acme of power and glory in the early part of his reign, found only trouble and perplexity at its close, and, being deposed by his sub-jects, died in seclusion.

Katherine Evans and Sarah Chevers, who started for Alexandria, did not meet with as favorable a reception, for on landing at Malta they were soon arrested by order of the Inquisition, and imprisoned in a small room where were only two holes for light and air. They were so oppressed by the heat that they frequently lay down on the floor by their door, hoping some air would come in at the threshold. Their skin was parched, the hair fell from their heads, and they often fainted. At last they were allowed to have the door open some part of the time each day. The inquisitors often visited them, endeavoring to persuade them to renounce their religion, and threatening them with death if they did not. But they were steadfast, and boldly expressed their views, confounding their opponents by the power and truth with which they vindicated their principles.

Notwithstanding all their trials, the peace of God so filled their hearts that they could write thus: "We do greatly rejoice and glorify the name of our Heavenly Father, though we be the least of the flock, yet we are of the true fold, whereof Christ Jesus is the Shepherd, and He hath a tender care over us, and hath carried us through and over our great afflictions.

We are witnesses He can provide a table in the wilderness, both temporal and spiritual. Oh the endless love of our God, who is as an everlasting fountain, whose crystal streams never cease running to every thirsty soul."

The rigor of their confinement was at last somewhat abated, and they preached Jesus zealously to all who came near them. After many fruitless attempts had been made for their release by their friends in England, George Fox went to the Earl of D'Aubeny, and represented the case in such strong terms that he promised to write to the authorities at Malta, requiring their release. This was accordingly effected, after three years of privation and suffering, during which these two frail, delicate women were enabled to exemplify the truth of the declaration, " My God shall supply all your need."

But it was in the New England Colonies that the extreme penalty of death was inflicted upon those whose greatest crime in the eyes of their judges was that they were Quakers. Mention has already been made of the persecutions to which some of this hated sect were subjected, and in 1655 the General Court of Plymouth issued a proclamation denouncing them as " publishing dangerous and horrid tracts," and declaring that any convicted of holding their views should be banished from the colony under pain of death. In obedience to this law four persons were ordered to leave the jurisdiction. They were William Robinson, Marmaduke Stephenson, William Leddra, and Mary Dyer, who had come to Boston to labor for their Lord. In obedience to this mandate they left the town, but William Robinson and Marmaduke Stephenson could not feel satisfied to go further than Salem. Here they spent the night with some of their friends, and in the morning, after an affecting parting, they started again for Boston with a few who resolved to bear them company. It seemed almost like a funeral procession, as they calmly but solemnly went to their doom, following what seemed to them the direction of their Lord. On reaching the town they were soon arrested and committed to prison. The next month Mary Dyer returned and was also taken into custody. The prisoners were then brought before the court and sentence of death pronounced upon them.

On the day appointed for their execution a band of two hundred armed men, besides many horsemen, were called out to escort these harmless, unarmed Quakers to the gallows. The prisoners were placed in the centre with a drummer next to them, who was ordered to make noise enough to drown their voices, if they attempted to speak to the crowds which followed them. There were mingled feelings in the hearts of the spectators, for all could not unite with the unjust judges, but the prisoners themselves were at peace. We are told " they went with great cheerfulness, as to an everlasting wedding feast." The men suffered first, and Mary Dyer ascended the scaffold, but as the rope was placed about her neck a cry was heard, " She is reprieved." Her son had made such earnest intercession that her life was granted him on condition she should leave the Colony at once.

The following letter will show that these sufferers acted in single-hearted obedience to their impressions of duty in thus, as it were, defying the rulers of Boston Colony.

LETTER OF WILLIAM ROBINSON TO GEORGE FOX.

" O beloved of the Lord, and highly esteemed and honored among the children of the Lord, who hath made thee a father unto thousands and hath given thee the spirit of wisdom and understanding, I was refreshed when I was constrained to write to give thee an account of our travels and labors in these countries."

After giving an account of the persecution and banishment of the Friends, he goes on to speak of himself : —

" Oh, God knows how near this went to me, when I did hear they had departed, and soon the Lord did lay it upon me to try their law ; yes, on the same day that I heard of their departure was I constrained, and soon made willing, to give up my life Boston's bloody laws to try, and was given up frequently in my spirit to the Lord's will, even to finish my testimony for the Lord against the town of Boston ; not knowing of any Friends to pass with me at that time, but the Lord had compassion on me, seeing how willingly I was given up to do His will, not counting my life dear to me, so that I might finish my course with joy; and on the day following, the Lord constrained my brother Marmaduke Stephenson to pass along with me to Boston, who is freely given up to suffer with me for the seed's sake, who doth dearly salute thee.

" O my dearly beloved, thou who art endued with power from on high, who art of quick discerning in the fear of our God ; oh remember us, — let thy prayers be put up unto the Lord God for us, that His power and strength may rest with us and upon us ; that faithful we may be preserved to the end. Amen.   WM. ROBINSON.

" From the Common Gaol in Boston,
the 12th of the Fifth Month, 1659."

In the spring of 1660 Mary Dyer felt she must return to Boston, and was soon in her old prison again. Being brought before the court, the governor, John Endicott, asked her if this was the same Mary Dyer, to which she replied, " I am." She then gave the reason for her return, that she believed the Lord had sent her to beseech them to repeal their wicked law, and to warn them that He would assuredly punish those who opposed His will. Her expostulations were unavailing, Governor Endicott was immovable, and she was condemned to be hung at nine o'clock the next day.

Morning came ; Boston Common presented an unwonted spectacle. Groups of awe-stricken women were talking in whispers of the sad fate awaiting one who was like themselves a wife and a mother. Children were gazing with wonder and terror at the gloomy gallows tree erected before them, and wondered what wicked thing this woman could have done that she must be hanged ; while strong men, who denounced the mistaken zeal of the Quakers, could but acknowledge they were an honest sect, and many would fain have let them alone. Soon came the sound of drum and fife, and a company of soldiers marched by; then came men beating their drums loudly, and by their side walked calmly and serenely the heroine of the day, the hated, despised Quaker. She ascended the scaffold, and when her life was again proffered, on condition she should leave Boston forever, she replied, " Nay, I cannot promise. In obedience to the will of the Lord I came, and in His will I abide, faithful unto death." The signal was given, the drop fell, and this faithful witness for Jesus went home to be with Him forever.

· These persecutions were soon stopped by the Home Government, and only one other person was hanged. When the Friends in England heard of these cruel deeds, Edward Burrough went to King Charles and told him " a vein of innocent blood was opened in his kingdom, which if it were not stopped would overrun all." The King had no great respect for the loyalty of his New England subjects, and expressed himself willing to put a stop to these proceedings at once. He accordingly wrote a mandamus ordering that no more Quakers should be persecuted,.but that they should be sent to the Home Government for trial. As no ship was likely soon to sail for New England, the Friends sent one at their own expense, to carry this important document. It was entrusted to Samuel Shattock, one of those who had been banished from Boston under pain of death.

When the ship arrived in Boston harbor, Governor Endicott and his associates were not a little surprised to see this banished man returning as the king's deputy, bringing his mandamus. There was, however, nothing to be done but to accept Samuel Shattock, and the ship-load of Quakers he brought with him, as peaceably as possible.

From this time persecution ceased in the New World, while in the Old the Friends were soon to be introduced into a school whose lessons were qualified to teach them to "endure hardness" like good soldiers of Jesus Christ.

In 1661 an Act of Conformity was passed by the King and Parliament forbidding the exercise of any other form of worship than the Protestant Episcopal. The order was also given that the oaths of supremacy and allegiance should be tendered to all whose loyalty was doubtful. Those who refused to take this oath were in danger of imprisonment for life and the loss of all their property.

This direct violation of the Declaration of Breda filled all non-conformists with alarm. Two thousand Presbyterian ministers were ejected from their homes in consequence, and the Friends again felt the pressure of persecution. Indeed, the blow fell more heavily upon them because of their conscientious opposition to all oaths. Four thousand members of the Society of Friends were thrown into prison; neither age nor sex was spared; old men with gray hair, and the young in the prime of life, were cast into loathsome dungeons. They believed the exercise of their public worship was a duty from which no man could discharge them, and continued their meetings. The magistrates and soldiery having closed many of their houses they were obliged to stand in the streets, where of course a crowd would soon gather. The ministers, taking advantage of this opening, declared the precious truths of the gospel with such power, that while some of the spectators mocked, others were constrained to say the Lord was with that people. It was not an unfrequent occurrence for a minister to be arrested while preaching and carried off to prison. Without hesitation another would take his place, and the order of the meeting was unbroken. The seed sown fell into some places where a plentiful harvest was afterwards gathered to the glory of God.

Even in these trying times the number of the Friends increased, and neither the danger of imprisonment, nor the cruel treatment experienced from the soldiery, could check the growth of the Society. Two boys, one sixteen, the other thirteen, were arrested at a meeting and brought before the Lieutenant of the Tower. He sent them to Bridewell, where their hands were placed in stocks, they were cruelly whipped and sent to prison, where they remained some time. Yet these undaunted lads wrote a letter from their prison house to the children of Friends, urging them to be faithful to their duty to the Lord, without regarding the power or malevolence of man. In some cases, where the parents and older Friends were imprisoned, the meetings were continued by the children, who, at the risk of sharing their suffering, met as they had been accustomed, to worship God.

CHAPTER IX.

ALTHOUGH King Charles had consented to the passage of the Act of Non-conformity, he sympathized so much with his Roman Catholic subjects that he sought to aid them. In 1662, with the consent of his Privy Council, he wrote a declaration of indulgence towards those, who, through conscientious scruples, could not conform to the Church of England. Parliament, however, steadily refused to accept this, or grant any indulgence to Dissenters, and as the king was sorely in need of subsidies he was obliged to yield to their decision. During the summer of 1663 the King and Queen visited some of the western counties of England, and while they were absent from London rumors were circulated of a conspiracy formed in the north, between the Republicans and Separatists, to raise a general insurrection. George Fox heard of this plot while traveling in Yorkshire, and knowing the danger to Friends from any public disturbance, he wrote and circulated a paper declaring the testimony of his people against any plots or conspiracies. A copy of this was sent to the King and Parliament. Notwithstanding this precaution Friends suffered severely ; their refusal to take any oath giving their enemies opportunity to denounce them as rebels against the government. The magistrates in Cumberland offered a crown a day to any one who would apprehend a Quaker preacher, and as George Fox was considered as the leader of the sect, a reward of five pounds was promised for his arrest.

After quite an extensive tour through Yorkshire, Cumberland, Durham, and Westmoreland, George Fox came to Swarthmore. Here he was informed that Colonel Kirby had, only a short time before, sent a lieutenant to the Hall to arrest him. He felt as he says, "moved of the Lord," to go to Kirby Hall and speak to its master. It was about five miles from Swarthmore, and on arriving there he found the reception room full of the gentry of the county. Nothing daunted by the company, he approached Colonel Kirby, saying he understood he wished to see him, and therefore had come to know what he had against him.

"Nothing," answered the Colonel, "but Mistress Fell must not keep great meetings at her house, for they meet contrary to the Act."

George Fox replied, that Act did not apply to them, but to those who met to plot and contrive and raise insurrections against the King, but, as Colonel Kirby knew, those who met at Margaret Fell's were his peaceable neighbors. After a friendly conversation Colonel Kirby shook him cordially by the hand, saying again he had nothing against him, and they parted.

The officials under Colonel Kirby were not so lenient, and taking advantage of his absence in London, the justices and deputy lieutenants met at Holker Hall, where Judge Preston lived, and granted a warrant to apprehend George Fox. Timely warning was sent to him, but he refused to escape, fearing if he did so the blow would fall more heavily upon those who were left. The next day an officer with sword and pistols came to Swarthmore Hall to arrest him. George Fox asked to see the order for his arrest, upon which the officer put his hand upon his sword, and refused to show any other warrant.

His friend Margaret Fell accompanied him to Holker Hall, where Sir George Middleton and others were assembled to try his case. The serious charge was brought against him that " he had written against the plotters, and had knocked them down." George Fox quaintly says, " this they could not make much of, for I told them I had heard of the plot, and had written against it."

Then said George Middleton, " You deny God, the church, and the faith." He replied, " Nay, I own God, the true church, and the true faith, but what church dost thou own ? "

As Middleton was a Romanist he could not answer that question, but turned upon the prisoner with these words, " You are a rebel and a traitor." George Fox quietly rose from his seat, and with great earnestness said : " I have suffered more than twenty such as thou or any present, I was imprisoned six months in the Derby dungeon, because I would not take up arms against the king at the battle of Worcester ; I was also sent a prisoner to Oliver Cromwell as a conspirator against him. Ye talk of a king, but how did ye all stand in the days of Cromwell, and what did ye do then for the king ? I have more love to him, and his eternal good and welfare, than any of you."

Justice Middleton now commanded that the oaths
of allegiance and supremacy should be put to him.
George Fox shrewdly asked whether he, who was himself a Catholic and a swearer, had taken the oath. " As
for us we cannot swear at all, because Christ and his
apostles have forbid it." This pointed query for the
moment warded off the blow; the oaths were dispensed
with, and the prisoner was released on his promise to
appear at the next Lancaster sessions.

True to his word, at the winter assizes George Fox
appeared at Lancaster. Among those upon the bench
were many noted opponents of Friends, one of whom,
Judge Fleming, had offered five pounds to any one
who would apprehend George Fox. The session was
large, but the crowd made way for the noted man
who was exciting so much attention. He quietly
walked up to his place, adhering to what he believed
to be his duty in not removing his hat, but saying,
" Peace be among you."

He was questioned in regard to the plot already
alluded to; but finding no grounds on which to establish any charges against him they again tendered him
the oaths. One of the justices asked him if he considered it unlawful to swear, an unwarrantable question, as no prisoner is obliged to criminate himself.

George Fox avoided the snare by saying, " In the
time of the law among the Jews before Christ came,
they were commanded to swear; but Christ who doth
fulfill the law, in these gospel times, commands not to
swear at all, and the Apostle James forbids swearing
even to them that were Jews and had the law of God."
He then produced a paper which he had written

against oaths, asking it should be read in open court, but this was refused, and he was remanded to prison for declining the oath. As he was led away, he said, "All people take notice that I suffer for the doctrine of Christ, and for obedience to His commands."

Lancaster jail was crowded with Quakers, some of them poor farmers, whose families were dependent upon them for support. Many of these had been zealous loyalists, and, before they adopted the peaceable views of Friends, had fought and bled for Charles I., and continued faithful to him to the end. Their persecutors were fierce Roundheads, who now professed a great zeal for the King, but whose conduct seemed to the prisoners to be very unjust and cruel. In some cases remonstrances effected the liberation of Friends, but most were suffered to lie in prison and many died there.

After three months' imprisonment George Fox was brought before the next quarter sessions, on the 14th of Third Month, 1664, and the first question put to him was "Will you take the oath of allegiance?" Without hesitancy came the bold answer, "I am a christian, and Christ commands me not to swear. Whether I should obey God or man judge ye."

After some further conversation, the judge said: "Well, George Fox, say whether thou wilt take the oath, yea or nay?"

In conscious innocence the prisoner replied, "If I could take any oath at all, I could take this; for I do not deny some oaths only, or on some occasions, but all oaths, according to Christ's doctrine, who hath commanded His followers 'Not to swear at all.' "Now if thou or any of you, or any of your ministers or priests here, will prove that ever Christ or His apostles, after they had forbidden all swearing, commanded Christians to swear then I will swear."

Several ministers were present, but none took up the gage thus boldly thrown down. The judge then told the jailer to take him away, the prisoner declaring: "It is for Christ's sake I cannot swear, and in obedience to His commands I suffer; and so the Lord forgive you all."

In the sixth month of this year, 1664, George Fox was again brought before Judge Turner. For two hours he stood among murderers and felons, the gazing-stock of the whole court. His indictment was read, and he showed so many errors in it that the judge was forced to confess he could not in justice be condemned from it. The unfailing snare, however, remained, and Judge Turner, starting up in a rage, exclaimed, "I can put the oath to any man here, and I will put it to you again." The Bible was handed to the prisoner, and he was asked whether he would take the oath or not. He replied, "You have given me a book to kiss and to swear on, and this book says, 'Kiss the Son,' and the Son saith in the book 'Swear not at all.' I say as the Book says, yet ye imprison me. How chance ye do not imprison the Book? How comes it the Book is at liberty among you, which bids me not to swear, yet ye imprison me for doing what the Book bids me?" "I held up the Bible open, to show them the place where Christ forbade swearing. They plucked the book out of my hand, and the judge said, Nay, but we will imprison George Fox."

Instead of obtaining his liberty by this clear exposure of the palpably gross errors of his indictment, he was reconducted to prison, there to be immured till the ensuing assizes; and in order to make his case still harder, his sufferings were increased tenfold by a second interference of Colonel Kirby, who gave particular orders to the jailer " to keep him close, and suffer no flesh alive to come at him, for he was not fit to be discoursed with by men." In consequence of this order he was removed into an upper chamber, in an old and ruinous tower of the castle, so much more dilapidated than his former abode that he was constantly exposed to the inclemencies of the weather, and often had the greatest difficulty to preserve his bed and clothing (which was always damp and cold) from being wet through. He was also so much distressed by smoke, which penetrated into his room from other fires in the prison, that at times he was nearly suffocated by it, and often could scarcely discern the light of a candle from its density. In this inhuman place he was doomed to pass the whole winter (which was unusually long and severe) for no crime, and was at last so much affected by a continued exposure to the cold and wet, and the constant inhaling of such an impure atmosphere, that he was reduced to a state of great suffering: his body became swollen, and his limbs so benumbed that he could with difficulty use them.

In this miserable dungeon George Fox remained a prisoner for eighteen months, when Colonel Kirby, and the magistrates who placed him there, feeling the odium of the exposure of their malice and hypocrisy, became desirous to have him removed from their neighborhood. Application was accordingly made to the King and council for his removal, under the plea that he " deserved no clemency or mercy." Yet the only thing that could be brought against him was his refusal to take an oath on account of religious scruples.

He was brought from his prison, his swollen limbs and emaciated appearance telling the story of his sufferings. Scarcely able to stand or walk he was placed on horseback and hurried away to Bentham, a distance of fourteen miles. One of the under jailers amused himself by lashing the horse, upon which the weary prisoner could scarcely sit, thus adding to his sufferings. He finally reached Scarborough Castle, where he was to spend the next year of his life, and was delivered into the custody of Sir Jordan Croslands, the governor, who, influenced no doubt by the misrepresentations of his persecutors, treated the poor, suffering prisoner with barbarous severity. At first he was put in a room with a sentry over him, but being very faint and weak, he was allowed sometimes to go out in the air with the sentry. He was afterwards removed to a room very open to the weather, and which smoked so much that it was but seldom he could have a fire. One day the governor came to see him, and George Fox lighted a little fire which immediately filled the room so full of smoke that the governor could hardly find his way out.

In order to render this little den habitable he expended fifty shillings in repairs, a sum of more importance in those days than now, but no sooner had he made it tolerable than they removed him to one much worse, where he had neither chimney nor hearth for fire, and into which the rain and wind beat, wetting both his clothes and bed. Having no fire at which to dry them, he became so benumbed by the damp and cold that his fingers swelled to double their usual size. He was so closely confined that his friends were not allowed to see him, or bring him the little comforts with which they would gladly have supplied him. Sometimes the soldiers would steal the few necessaries he sent for, from the person who brought them. For a long time his food consisted of nothing but bread, and his drink, water in which he had steeped a little wormwood. Commonly, he says, " a three penny loaf served me three weeks, and sometimes longer."

During this long period of suffering he had an opportunity for practicing the lessons he had learnt in the school of Christ, and, through the grace of God strengthening him, he was enabled to manifest christian patience and fortitude, and still adorn the doctrine of God his Saviour. While debarred from the privilege of seeing his friends, others were allowed entrance into his prison, many of whom came to tantalize him, and some to question his religious views. Always ready to give a reason for the hope that was in him, George Fox gladly availed himself of the opportunity of declaring the truth as it is in Jesus. His christian conduct at last had an influence upon the governor and his officers, and they came to treat him with respect, and even with kindness.

While George Fox was thus suffering for conscience'

sake his kind hostess, the widow of Judge Fell, was in her turn subjected to trial and imprisonment. One day as the Friends were quietly sitting in their meeting in Swarthmore Hall, Colonel Kirby made his appearance and took down the names of all the men present. A few days after an officer came to bring Margaret Fell before a special meeting of the magistracy, assembled at Ulverstone. She was questioned in regard to the meetings held at her house, and told if she would not promise to discontinue them, they would tender her the oaths of allegiance and supremacy. She replied, so long as the Lord let her have a house, she would in spirit and in truth endeavor to worship God in it. The oath was then tendered, and as she could not conscientiously take any oaths, she, too, was sent to prison till the next assizes. Here the same plan was pursued with the same result. She could neither take the oath, nor accept her liberty on condition of giving up the meetings at her house, and so was remanded for three months more. At the expiration of this period Judge Turner passed sentence of premunire against her, by which she was outlawed, condemned to imprisonment for life, and her property confiscated to the Crown. But neither faith nor courage forsook her, and she returned this answer to her cruel sentence : " Although I am out of the king's protection, I am not out of the protection of the Almighty God."

The Lord did indeed sustain her, as she parted from her children, and returned to her gloomy prison, not knowing whether she should ever see them or her beloved home again. She proved, of a truth, that

" Stone walls do not a prison make
Nor iron bars a cage."

for the light of the Lord shone in her heart, and His peace filled her soul.

Shut up in Lancaster Castle, Margaret Fell, though debarred from active coöperation with her friends, was able to use her pen in the service of her Master. She sent letters of advice and counsel to the different meetings of Friends, and tracts on various subjects came from her dungeon walls, flying like seed-vessels of truth, in many cases to spring up and bear fruit to God's glory. After three years' imprisonment she wrote a forcible appeal to the king, reminding him of the declaration of Breda, and his promise to her that if the Friends were peaceable they should be protected. She also referred to her interview with the king, and her advice to him to beware of taking counsel of those who would cppress them whose only crime was that they obeyed and worshipped the Lord Jesus. She then describes her prison as " a place where storm, wind, and rain found easy access, and which sometimes was filled with smoke."

This remonstrance had no effect, and she remained in her gloomy prison-house nearly two years longer, when the efforts of her friends on her behalf were successful. In 1668 she was released from her confinement, and allowed to return to her home and children after an imprisonment of nearly five years.

CHAPTER X.

WHILE George Fox was shut up in prison the sufferings of Friends were greatly increased by the passage of the Act, justly called the " Infamous Conventicle Act." This declared that " any person of the age of sixteen and upwards, who should be found at any meeting or conventicle, under color or pretense of any exercise of religion, in any other manner than is allowed by the liturgy of the Church of England; at which meetings should be five persons or more assembled over and above those of the same household, should be fined £5 on the first offense, or be imprisoned for a term not exceeding three months;" for a second offense £10 and an imprisonment of not more than six months, while the punishment of the third was to be transportation for seven years. This law went into effect on the 1st of Seventh Month, 1664, and excited the just animadversion of the more thoughtful people of England. Its interference with the privacy of domestic life; its encouragement of eaves-droppers and informers; and the probable result of sending out of the country citizens of good moral repute, industrious, and contributing to the public wealth, were set forth, and those in power warned that such wickedness would sooner or later bring the judgments of God upon the people. It was intended, apparently, for all non-conformists, but was rarely enforced against any but Friends, who were soon crowded into the prisons because they would not relinquish their liberty of conscience.

One of their number, George Whitehead, proclaimed in a pamphlet issued at this time: " Since then our meetings are kept in obedience to the Lord God, and according to the freedom He hath given us, we may not leave off our testimony for God in that case, but we must be faithful to Him, whatsoever we suffer on that account." Taking advantage of their faithfulness in the performance of this duty, the magistrates hastened their proceedings in order that the nation might be delivered from the supposed dangerous people, whose presence was so obnoxious. After breaking up a meeting, those in attendance would be sent to prison for a few days, and when set at liberty, being found at their meetings again, the same course was pursued, and before the 12th of Eighth Month, only six weeks after the passage of the Act, eight persons were arraigned for the third offense. Their indictment was brought before the grand jury, who could not agree on a verdict and ignored the bill. The judge, however, insisting on a reconsideration of their opinion, they brought in a verdict against the prisoners. The judge then told the Friends that if they would promise to go to no more meetings they might be released. This, of course, they could not do, and were accordingly sentenced to be transported beyond the seas, — some to the island of Barbadoes, and others to Jamaica.

A fresh difficulty now arose, for the captains of vessels sailing to these ports were unwilling to take any such passengers. One was at last compelled to take them on board his ship, which was tossed about by contrary winds, and could make no progress. After cruising about for two months, the captain and the sailors became so uneasy that they landed the unoffending Quakers at Deal, giving them a certificate declaring that they did not run away, but were freely set on shore by the captain, who added, " I . durst not go off with these prisoners, because I found them to be honest men, who did not deserve banishment."

The Friends returned to their homes, and by letter acquainted the King and Council with the whole proceeding. This letter was read at the council board, and they were remanded to prison till some one could be found to take them away. After an imprisonment of seven years the King ordered their release.

Two hundred were sentenced to banishment in this and the succeeding year, but the same difficulty continued, and only seventeen were really sent away. The remainder were kept in the already crowded prisons, where many laid down their lives for the sake of their religion. Yet the supporting power of their God was with them, as will be seen by an extract of a letter from one who was sentenced to Jamaica. " There is no God like unto our God, who is come nigh unto us in a needful time, and is present with us, to refresh and warm our hearts." Their constancy is shown in the answer of a woman, when asked what she had to say to the evidence given against her. " If I had as many bodies as hairs on my head, I could lay them all down for the living eternal truth of the living God."

As the year 1664 drew to a close persecution continned to increase, and the new year opened gloomily. The King declared he neither wished to see the Quakers, or to hear from them, as he could do nothing more for them; and as the Friends went on First-day morning to attend their place of worship, none of them knew whether he would ever again see his home and his loved ones. Yet while these severe measures were exacted for forcing uniformity in religious matters, true religion was never more neglected. The manners and habits of the age were corrupt and immoral. The profligacy of the court was repeated among the common people, and "drunkenness, profane swearing, and debauchery abounded in the nation."

Many remonstrances and prophetic warnings were sent to the King and Parliament, by earnest Friends who felt constrained of the Lord to warn them of His judgments.

One was written by George Fox " the Younger," as he was called, to distinguish him from the veteran now lying in Scarborough Castle. As early as 1661 he mourns over the judgments that are coming upon England, saying the Lord had spoken to him concerning the inhabitants. " An overflowing scourge, yea, even a great scourge, yea, even a great and terrible judgment, will come upon the land, and many in it will fall and be taken away."

Another Friend wrote the following laconic epistle, addressed to the King and both Houses of Parliament.

" Meddle not with my people, because of their
conscience to me, and banish them not out of the
nation because of their conscience, for if you do, I
will send my plagues upon you, and ye shall know
that I am the Lord.

" Written in obedience to the Lord by His servant,

" GEORGE BISHOP."

In the early part of the year 1665 two great evils
fell upon the English nation, in which it was scarcely
surprising Friends should see the hand of the Lord,
in chastisement, upon a sinful and persecuting people.
The war with Holland, wantonly commenced by the
English court, and promoted by the selfishness of
France, brought with it the inevitable results of
broken hearts, the sacrifice of valuable lives, and
money worse than wasted.

But this was not all; as the early months of the
year passed, there came from city and hamlet a deep
cry of terror, " The plague has broken out." Amid
the festivities of the court there walked an unbidden
guest, carrying fear and anguish into many hearts.
Ruthlessly laying his hand alike on rich and poor,
young and old, his path was strewn with his victims,
which in five months were estimated at one hundred
thousand.

Business in London was neglected, the merchant
left his store and went home to die, the artisan
ceased his work, the King and his courtiers fled to
Oxford, and half the houses in the city were marked
with the ominous tablet, " The Lord have mercy on
us." Grass grew in the populous streets except on

those which led to the grave-yards, and the busy .
hum of life and pleasure gave place to the mournful
trappings of death and woe.   At first the interments
were only at night, but the number of deaths increased so rapidly, that the hoarse ´call was heard at
all hours, " Bring out your dead."

> " How sunk the inmost heart of all,
>   As rolled the dead-cart slowly by,
>   With creaking wheel, and harsh hoof fall,
>   The dying turned him to the wall
>   To hear it, and to die."

- But notwithstanding this fearful visitation the
persecution of the non-conformists proceeded with
unrelenting vigor, and the Five Mile Act was introduced and passed at Oxford.   In the preamble to
this bill it was declared, that " the non-conformist
ministers instilled principles of schism and rebellion
into the people."   The bill enacted that it should be
penal for " any non-conformist minister to teach in
a school, or come within five miles (except as a trav-
eler in passing) of any city, burough, or corporate
town, or any place whatever, in which he had
preached or taught, since the passing of the Act of
Uniformity, before he has subscribed to the afore-
mentioned oath, before a magistrate, etc., under a
penalty of £40."   One third of this sum was to be
paid to the informer.   Though this law was ostensi-
bly aimed at the clergy of the Presbyterians, Baptists,
and Independents, it was nevertheless principally
made use of in distressing Friends.

The committals to Newgate continued until the
plague broke out within its walls, when the King,

urged by the physicians, ordered that no more persons should be sent there. Within those dreary walls there was much suffering endured, however, with a truly christian spirit. The following testimony is borne by George Whitehead, who remained in London during this terrible season to minister to the comfort of his imprisoned brethren: " When sorrow and sadness have seized upon my spirit, at their sad sufferings, this has refreshed me, that Christ their salvation and redemption was manifest to and in them. With such to live was Christ, even in this state, and to die was gain, it being through death, that the Lord had appointed the final deliverance of many from the cruelties and rod of their oppressors."

The King one day inquired whether " any Quakers had died of the distemper? " An affirmative reply induced him to say, " Then they can't say that the plague is a punishment sent for their enemies, because of having imprisoned them, when they are dying of it themselves." But the Puritan idea of the national punishment for national sins was not extinct in England, and many besides Friends, mourning over the sins and corruption of the day, saw in this calamity the visitation of an offended God.

The widows and orphans whose homes were rendered desolate by the plague, now claimed the attention of the Society always ready to assist their suffering companions. A number of Friends, both men and women, devoted themselves to the work of administering relief, holding regular meetings once a week, and devising means of meeting the need of the cases presented. Those residing in the country contributed of their substance, and also gave their personal service.

But to return to the lonely prisoner in Scarborough Castle, shut in by the permission of God from all participation in either the danger of the plague, or the opportunity of relieving distress. His service was to show to those around the power of a living Christ, bearing patiently all the thorn-pricks of life, and drawing sweetness from the bitterness of his lot, by the wondrous alchemy of a Saviour's love manifested in him. And such a living epistle was he in his prison cell that at his release, which soon came, this character was given of him by the officers: " He is as stiff as a tree, and as pure as a bell, for we never could bow him."

After an imprisonment of a year George Fox wrote to the King, giving an account of his long confinement, and through the efforts of his friend Esquire Marsh, an order for his release was sent the first day of Ninth Month, 1666. The governor parted kindly from him, and ever after assisted Friends whenever it was in his power.

The very day after George Fox left his prison-house the city of London was visited by another calamity, scarcely less terrible than the dreaded plague. It had been a very hot summer, and the houses in London, being mostly built of timber filled in with plaster, were dry and combustible as firewood. In the middle of the night a fire broke out near London Bridge in a baker's shop, where a quantity of fagots was stored, and in a few moments the flames spread from house to house, baffling all attempts to check their progress. For three days the fire fiend sped on his way, devouring the richest warehouses, the finest churches, and the abodes of the nobility, as well as the humble dwellings of the poor. When at last he ceased his mad course, two thirds of that populous city lay a sightless mass of cinders and ashes. The scene is thus described by Evelyn in his " Diary : " " The sky was of a fiery aspect, like the top of a burning oven, the light being seen above forty miles around for many nights. The conflagration was so universal, and the people so astonished, that from the beginning they hardly stirred to quench it ; so that there was nothing heard or seen but crying out and lamentation, and running about like distracted creatures."

Only the day but one before the fire broke out, there had been a strange sight in the crowded, busy streets of the city. A Friend from Huntingdonshire passed through them, with his doublet unbuttoned, rushing about frantically, scattering his money, and crying out that the people of that city should do so in a few days. No one believed his prediction, but it was fully verified at the time of the fire.

During the time of the Commonwealth there were other instances of Friends denouncing woes, and behaving in what would now be considered an unseemly manner. In the calmer atmosphere in which we live we can scarcely understand such actions, but, as has been well said, " we shall not prove ourselves to be more enlightened than the men of those times, by ridiculing their weaknesses, and overlooking the strength and nobility of their characters. It seems a strange world to us, but this was the world in which Fox and those who had similar aims moved, and if we would endeavor to understand their real character, and the real bearing of their actions, we must by an effort of imagination throw ourselves into the spirit of the times." [1]

[1] Barclay's *Inner Life of Commonwealth.*

CHAPTER XI.

WHEN George Fox was released from his rigorous imprisonment in Scarborough Castle, he found signs of trouble in the church he loved so well. After attending a few meetings, which he records as " blessed seasons," he turned his steps towards London, arriving there to find the crowded city a ruin, and two thirds of its inhabitants homeless, their dwellings having been burned to ashes. He himself was weak in body, his limbs swollen with cruel hardships. His early companions, the valiant sixty who had gone out two by two to preach the gospel, were either dead or in prison, and the congregations they had been the means of gathering had been sifted by persecution or were suffering from internal dissensions. It was evident to this wise, clear-headed man, that some course must be taken by which the different gatherings of the Friends might be united in one harmonious whole.

" It cannot be said that any system of dicipline formed a part of the original compact of the Society. There was not, indeed, to human appearance anything systematic in its formation. It was an association of persons who were earnestly seeking a saving knowledge of Divine Truth. They were men of prayer, and diligent searchers of the Holy Scriptures. Unable to find rest in the various systems of religion then

professed by the christian world, they believed they
found the Truth in a more full reception of Christ,
not only as the living and ever-present Head of the
church in its aggregate capacity, but also as the light
and life, — the spiritual teacher, ruler, and friend of
every individual member." [1]   Their previous belief
in the doctrine of the manhood of Christ, in His pro-
pitiatory sacrifice, mediation, and intercession, was as
precious to them as ever.

The views of Friends in regard to the Headship of
Christ in their meetings, were entirely opposed to
the prevailing idea that one man's performance on
the part of others was essential to public worship;
and consequently separated those who united with
them from those who adhered to the old system. This
separation would naturally unite in communities those
whose views were the same, and thus little churches
sprung up whose membership was merely the bond of
religious unity and fellowship.   As the members increased some regular arrangement for the preservation of order was found to be needful, and general
meetings for conference were held at an early date.
Allusion to one of these held at Skipton has been
made.   At these gatherings an account was given of
the " prosperity and spreading of the Lord's blessed
Truth," and of the laborers who were " moved of the
Lord to go beyond the seas, " for no one went out on
their Master's service without acquainting the Yearly
Meeting of their desire, and so " all went in the unity
of the church of Christ and the power of the Lord."
A collection was also recommended to be taken up

[1] *Book of Extracts of London Yearly Meeting.*

in all the smaller meetings for the use of these laborers while on their different missions.

The necessary care for this work occupying so much time, these details were finally left to the Yearly Meeting, and the General Meetings afterwards held were for the preaching of the gospel and building up of the church. The following minute will show the care felt by the early Friends, not unduly to secure tables on occasions like these.

" From Friends met in Durham, to Friends who shall meet at Skipton, Eighth Month, 5th, 1659."

" Dear Friends, these things being agreed in clearness of Truth, which hitherto have taken up much time at the General Meetings to the loss of many precious opportunities, you will see greater things before you which more chiefly concerns the state of the church, and will be of greater service to the Truth."

In 1672 it was agreed that " for the better ordering, managing, and regulating of the public affairs of Friends" it would be advisable to hold one meeting annually in London, composed of representatives from different places. Since the year 1678 this has been held with unbroken regularity. The interest and care felt by George Fox in this meeting, and his ideas of the duties of its members, will be seen by the following letter addressed to it in 1689.

" Dear Friends, be faithful in the service of God, and mind the Lord's business. Be diligent, and bring the power of the Lord over all that have gainsaid it. And you that are faithful, go to visit all that have been convinced from house to house, that if it be possible you may not leave an hoof in Egypt. And so

every one of you go seek the lost sheep and bring him
on your back to the fold, and there will be more joy
over that one sheep than of the ninety and nine in
the fold." [1]

Quarterly meetings were also held in the various
counties, and in the city of London, where there
seemed still greater need, a Two Weeks Meeting is
spoken of. The object of these meetings is well de-
fined by Edward Burrough in a paper written in
1662. After alluding to the blessing of the Lord
upon the labors of the ministers in London, and the
consequent increase of the church, he speaks of the
many occasions in which care was requisite, such as
" providing convenient meeting places for the publishing of truth, and how the poor people that believed should be honestly taken care of, that no want
should be amongst them, that the sick, weak, and im-
potent should be visited and provided for, and that
such servants as were put away out of their services
for receiving the truth should be looked after, and
placed in some honest employments." As in the early
christian church, it was considered by him that it
was not meet that those who were entrusted with
the ministry of the word should " serve tables."
Consequently he goes on to propose that " the men
Friends of the city, or the ancientest of them in the
truth (not excluding any), should meet together at
the Bull and Mouth, once in a fortnight, or once a
month, as they in the wisdom of God should find it
necessary, for the management of Truth's affairs."
Thus, he adds, " ye in your places according to your

[1] *Internal Religious Life of Commonwealth*, Robert Barclay.

6

gifts, as well as we in our callings to which we were ordained and sent forth, should be helpful and assistant one to another." He gives this caution at the close, which shows how fully the early Friends indorsed the declaration of the Apostle Paul: " For ye are members one of another," and "if one member suffer, all the members suffer with it."

" If there be any spirit of slighting or contempt on your part of the ministry and ministers of the gospel, or if on our part do arise any lordliness or self-seeking over and among the flock of Christ, this kind of spirit is not from above, but is devilish, and its effects will be destructive, and bring the wrath of the Lord against such as shall ever give place to it."

During the first eleven years of the existence of the Society in London no further organization was requisite, but at the period of which we now speak some further means were necessary to exercise due care over so large an area as the London district presented.

" I was moved of the Lord," says George Fox in his journal, under date of 1666, " to recommend the setting up of five Monthly Meetings in London to take care of God's glory, to admonish and exhort such as walked disorderly or carelessly and not according to Truth. For whereas Friends had only Quarterly Meetings, and had now grown so numerous, I was moved to recommend the setting up of Monthly Meetings throughout the nation." The necessity for watchful care over such as walked carelessly was becoming apparent, as will be seen from an account given by a Friend to George Fox of one of the meetings in London. " Truly, George, they are a very poor, divided company, and several very bad spirits among them, and very unruly, and not subject one to another." The multitude gathered by the fervor of the early preachers needed to be molded into an orderly and regular society. The cruel laws against their mode of worship acted like a fan in winnowing the chaff from the wheat ; but there were many instances of an outward profession unaccompanied by the fruits of a religious life and conversation.

The rectifying of these disorders became a prominent feature in the business of the Monthly Meetings, and a great reformation was wrought by them. George Fox thus speaks of their beneficial effects : " Since these meetings have been settled, many mouths have been opened in thanksgiving, and have blessed the Lord God that He did ever send me forth on this service. For now all are coming to have a care for God's honor and glory, and all to see that those who profess the truth do walk in the truth, and order their conversation aright. And as all having this care upon them, and are exercised in His Holy Spirit, they may come to know and partake of the government of Christ, the First and the Last, the Beginning and the Ending, the Foundation of God, Christ Jesus, the Amen."

In the minutes of the Yearly Meeting of 1676 we find the qualification for membership in these meetings. " All the faithful men and women in every country, city, and nation, whose faith stands in the power of God, the gospel of Christ, and have received this gospel, and are in possession of this gospel, the power of God, they have a right to the power of this meeting, for they be heirs of the power and authority of the men's and women's meetings." All such were admitted to these disciplinary meetings, or, if they were children of members and deemed converted, they were invited to attend the meetings for business. In that early day there was an outside membership of those professing with Friends, who were entitled to pastoral oversight, and, in case of necessity, to pecuniary aid and relief, but who were not considered competent to exercise the discipline of the church, which was vested in the hands of more experienced Friends. Conversion to Christ was the distinction. If any one was deemed by the elders to be converted he was invited to a participation in the meetings for discipline, if only convinced he was merely a participator in church privileges. Robert Barclay speaks very clearly on this subject: " To be a member of any particular church of Christ, as this inward work is indispensably necessary, so is also the outward profession and belief in Jesus Christ and those holy truths delivered by Him."

All these meetings were conducted by men, but George Fox, remembering that all are one in Christ Jesus, was desirous of elevating the female sex by recognizing them as helpers in spiritual as well as temporal things. His enlightened view was " that faithful women called to a belief of the truth, and made partakers of the same precious faith, and heirs of the same everlasting gospel of life and salvation as the men are, might in like manner come into the profession and practice of the gospel order, and therein be meet helps to the men in the restoration, in the service of the truth, and the affairs of the church, as they are outwardly in civil and temporal things ; that so all the family of God, women as well men, might know, possess, and perform their offices and services in the house of God." [1]

Some time before this, according to Gilbert Latey, the men Friends found much pressing upon them in the care of the sick, of the orphans and widows, and the families of those who were shut up in prison, and called in the aid of the women, " for we could no longer do without their help and assistance." Women formed a large proportion of the Six Weeks Meeting, and when Monthly Meetings were first established, it was the practice for the women to sit with the men, and the business was transacted jointly. " Thus the women shared in the discipline with the men, but without any separate meetings for it." [2] It afterwards became the custom to hold a joint meeting for worship, after which the men and women separated to attend to the business of the church. Thus in that day, when the position of woman was not as exalted as now, the broad, liberal views of the founder of this society acknowledged her as a fellow-laborer with man in the service of the gospel.

For the government of these meetings for discipline, George Fox drew up a paper, which is to be found entered in manuscript on most of the books of the London meetings. This paper is interesting, as

[1] *Friends' Library*, vol. i.
[2] *London Friends' Meetings*.

containing the germ of much of the subsequent disciplinary action of the Society. Directions were given as to the proper care in regard to marriage; the watchful training of children; the registration of births, deaths, and marriages; care over those who were suffering for conscience' sake; and exhortations to honesty, morality, and sobriety. Provision was also made by which those who refused to comply with these rules were to be cut off from membership. George Fox was a lover of order, and resolutely encountered and defeated all evidences of that spirit which would make the liberty of the truth degenerate into license, yet a spirit of tenderness is breathed through his writings. In one of his epistles he says: "All who behold their brother or sister in transgression, go not in a rough, light, or upbraiding spirit, to reprove or admonish him or her, but in the power of the Lord and the spirit of the Lamb and in the wisdom and love of the truth to admonish such an offender." If the care and labor of the church proved unavailing in reclaiming the offender, he was to be disunited from the society; but this was only to be resorted to after long and patient labor. Nor did the care of the Monthly Meeting end here, for after disownment the offender was still to be visited, and if he could be convinced of his error and prevailed upon to sign a paper of condemnation of his course, the arms of the church were lovingly opened to welcome him back.

Another meeting, of a more select character and acting as a sort of court of appeal from the more public Two Weeks or Monthly Meeting, was called the Six Weeks Meeting.

The records of this meeting commence in 1671, and the names of the Friends composing it are appended to the first minute under date, Eighth Month, 28th. Forty-nine men and thirty-five women Friends composed it; "grave and antient" they were called, though many of them were in the vigor of middle life. They were probably chosen by George Fox himself, who calls this meeting the "prime meeting of the city." He gives the following directions for its guidance: "The Six Weeks Meeting is for to see that all their meetings are preserved by the wisdom of God in the unity of the Spirit, the bond of peace, and in the fellowship of the Holy Ghost, being ordered by the pure, peaceable, gentle, heavenly Wisdom, easy to be entreated, holy and virtuous examples to all other meetings, both in city and country. And that all may be careful to speak short and pertinent to matters, in a christian spirit, and despatch business quickly, and to keep out of long debates and heats, and, with the Spirit of God, keep that down which is doting about questions and strife of words, that tends to parties and contention, — not to speak more than one at a time, nor any in a fierce way, for that is not to be allowed in any society, neither natural nor spiritual, but as the Apostle says, ' Be swift to hear, slow to speak,' and let it be in the Grace which seasons all words."

This meeting was also a means for dispensing assistance to the needy. In 1673 one John Goodson, a surgeon, offers to the meeting "to take a large house for distempered and discomposed persons." There are also frequent entries on the minutes of money voted or collections ordered to relieve distress in various parts of the world. To Friends in Holland and Holstein, the captive Friends in Algiers, and the sufferers for conscience' sake in Dantzig, Emden, etc. And besides their own people, they also remembered the stranger within their gates. A Dane, a Spaniard, a Silesian widow, were relieved by this meeting; and in 1693, we find the following minute evidencing their wide-spread sympathies: " Friends having under their consideration the poor condition of the Pietists now in England, about forty, the Friends undernamed are desired to draw up a few lines to be read in the public meetings at the conclusion thereof, next First Day, for a collection for their relief." This Six Weeks Meeting, under somewhat different organization, is still held in London.

In addition to these meetings for the care of the members in general, one other must be mentioned which was held in London from the earliest rise of the Society. This was a conference of ministers only, in regard to their work, and for their mutual counsel and encouragement. It was held at first in a private house, and was afterwards removed to the Bull and Mouth. As early as eight o'clock on First Day morning the men ministers in London gathered in an " upper room," while a number of horses were tethered in the street near by. After a time of waiting upon the Lord for guidance, the needs of the different meetings in the city and its neighborhood were mentioned, and the ministers separated each to the place to which he was called, either directly by the Lord speaking in his heart, or by the voice of his brethren. On Second Day they again assembled to give an account of their labor and the condition in which they found the flock. Thus the different meetings were supplied with ministers, and an over-plus in any one was prevented by this watchful care. The early Friends, while magnifying the office of the Holy Spirit as the Teacher of His people, were also fully convinced that instrumental means are used in promulgating the gospel, and were careful that the gifts bestowed by the Lord upon His children should be used to His glory.

The arrangements so methodically made were entered in books which still remain, and for a long time the only acknowledgment of a minister was the introduction of his name into this book of records.[1] Some years later this meeting was enlarged by the addition of elders, and the name of the Morning Meeting is still continued in London. Its duties were increased and the care of the ministry came more especially under the meetings for ministers and elders which were afterwards held.

These ministers' meetings were a source of vast energy, as might be expected from such a gathering of earnest working christians, apportioning to themselves the home missionary and church work, according to the grace received by the different individuals. A watchful care was maintained over the health of the body, while their own spiritual life was increased by waiting upon the Lord. A minute of one of those meetings held in 1698 is worthy of notice.

[1] *London Friends' Meetings.*

6*

" At our meeting of Friends in the ministry, and elders, in the meeting-house in Chesterfield, these things following passed: First, in our waiting upon the Lord, the Lord appeared very sweetly and powerfully among us, and in us, to our great comfort; Praises to His name forever! Secondly, we had a precious time of prayer and supplication to the Lord, in a sweet stream and current of Life Eternal! Thirdly, after prayer, we, every one that had a part in the ministry, declared how it had been with us, as to our faithfulness herein, and where we had found by experience that the enemy had hurt us, or overtaken us unawares at times. Fourthly, the snares, baits, gins, traps, and nets of the enemy were spoken of, and laid to view; and caution, counsel, and advice in the love of God given freely from Him amongst us." [1]

After the meetings in London were satisfactorily established, the same care was exercised over the other parts of England, Scotland, Ireland, and Wales. This required much time and many laborious journeys, which were no small trial; in the feeble condition of George Fox. At length the object was accomplished, and meetings for discipline were instituted throughout the kingdom. He also wrote letters to Friends in Holland, Barbadoes, and several parts of America, recommending the same practice.

The children of his people next engaged his attention, and he advised the setting up of schools for their instruction. While deprecating undue reliance upon human learning, he realized most fully that the

[1] *Inner Life of Commonwealth.*

talents bestowed upon man were to be cultivated,
and as many Friends were too poor or too much
harassed by persecution to contribute much towards
the education of their children, he recommended the
church to take this care. Two boarding-schools
were instituted, one for boys at Waltham, and one
for girls at Shackwell, for instructing them, to use
his own words, " in whatsoever things were civil and
useful in the creation."

While George Fox was thus engaged in building
up and molding into a compact body the church he
had been instrumental in gathering, it must not be
supposed he was the only one thus engaged. He
had able coadjutors, as much interested as himself in
the welfare of their loved Society; but so long as he
lived all paid, as it were, an instinctive deference to
him and to his authority in the church. That this
was not of his own seeking is evident from his epistles, where he declares his object to be to bring his
friends, "not to myself, but to His glory that sent
me, and when I turned you to Him that is able to
save you, I left you to Him." Of course there were
those, as we shall see hereafter, who opposed him
and impugned his motives; but leaving them to the
Lord, he pursued his way with humility and moderation.

The year 1666 was noticeable for sharp and bitter
persecution to the Friends, notwithstanding which
their numbers continued to increase. Two men
joined their ranks this year who occupied a high po-
sitiou in a worldly point of view, and who became
eminently useful to the Society. These were Robert

Barclay, the son of Colonel David Barclay of Ury, and William Penn, son of Admiral Penn. A little glimpse of their former lives may be interesting.

Colonel David Barclay had been a soldier under Gustavus Adolphus, King of Sweden, and until he was past middle life had shown his bravery on many a battle-field. But neither the applause of men, nor the comforts of social life by which he was surrounded, could satisfy him, and turning from the hypocrisy of the world he sought something more durable. Hearing there was a people called Quakers, who were honest and truthful, he thought their religion must be different from that of other professors. He took occasion to converse with some of the Friends, and was convinced their principles were correct. During an imprisonment in Edinburgh Castle, after the restoration of King Charles, his views were confirmed by intercourse with some Friends also confined there, and he resolved to join the Society. He emerged from his prison no longer the brave soldier of an earthly king, but an equally brave follower of the Prince of Peace, and found it necessary to exercise both faith and patience in enduring the scorn and contumely this change brought upon him.

His son Robert was sent to Paris for his education, and made such progress in his studies as to attract the attention of his masters. His uncle, with whom he was placed, was proud of the talents of his young nephew, and would fain have adopted him as his child. But his father, feeling afraid of the influence of the Roman Catholic religion on the tender mind of his son, sent for Robert to return to Scotland. This was in his seventeenth year, two years before his father joined the Friends. The next three years were spent in study and mental improvement, but another subject also engrossed his attention. He saw the change in his father's views, and was impressed with his circumspect life ; but no effort was made unduly to influence his own views. Indeed, instrumental means do not seem to have been much used in turning him towards Friends, but as he earnestly sought the truth the Lord showed him the way in which he should walk, and before he was twenty years old he too had cast in his lot with the Friends. For the remainder of his life he labored abundantly with both tongue and pen, seeking to bring others to a knowledge of the truth as it is in Jesus, and to defend the true christian divinity as he understood it to be set forth in the Holy Scriptures. In the latter part of his short life he was chosen Governor of East Jersey in North America, and the appointment was confirmed by King Charles II. The Royal Commission states: " Such are his known fidelity and capacity that he has the government during life, but no other governor after him shall have it longer than three years." He never assumed the office in person, the duties being performed by a deputy, and he died in his own house at Ury in great peace with the Lord, in the forty-second year of his age.

It was in Ireland that William Penn first formed acquaintance with the Friends. Thomas Loe, a minister from England, was at the meetings in Cork, and Admiral Penn, then residing there, sent for him to come to his house. His preaching had such an effect upon the whole family that William, then only a boy of eleven, never quite forgot it. When at Oxford, four years afterwards, he again met with Thomas Loe, who held some meetings there. His serious impressions were deepened and he would fain have joined the Friends. It was no part of his father's plan that his son should be a despised Quaker, and many efforts were made to turn him from that purpose. All, however, were unavailing, and in the twenty-fourth year of his age he became a minister of the Society of Friends, and through a long life faithfully served his Master. Before Admiral Penn died his views were very much changed, and he confessed that his son had been wise in choosing the service of Christ, rather than the applause of the world.

CHAPTER XII.

THE honored mistress of Swarthmore Hall was all these long years shut up within the walls of Lancaster Castle, in a place which she thus describes: " The storm and wind and rain find easy access, and which sometimes is filled with smoke." Deprived of active coöperation with her friends, she found solace in the use of her pen. By her position in society and her strong, vigorous mind she had always exercised a commanding influence in the little body among whom she had cast her lot, by whom she was regarded as a mother in Israel; and now in her captivity she continned a loving oversight over the infant church, and epistles of advice and counsel found their way to the different meetings of Friends. She also wrote several tracts, and an earnest and forcible letter to the king, expostulating with him for his violation of the Declaration of Breda, and his promise to her that Friends should not be molested if they lived peaceably. Charles II., however, took no notice of this appeal, and she remained in prison nearly two years longer, when the persevering efforts of her friends obtained her release in 1668, after an imprisonment of four years and a half.

She did not long remain in her comfortable home, for very soon we find her engaged in visiting all the prisons in England where any Friends were confined.

She had learned by sad experience the trials and privations experienced by those who were incarcerated in the dismal jails of that day, and longed to comfort the prisoners. And having also proved the supporting power of the Lord, she was well fitted to be a minister of consolation, and brought a ray of brightness to many a lonely, sorrowing one.

A year was spent in this service, and at its close an event took place of much importance to George Fox and herself, which he thus describes : —

" I had seen from the Lord a considerable time before that I should take Margaret Fell to be my wife. And when I first mentioned it to her she felt the answer of Life from God thereunto. But though the Lord had opened this thing to me, yet I had not received the command of the Lord for the accomplishment of it then. Whereto I let the thing rest, and went on in the work and service of the Lord as before, according as he led me, traveling up and down this nation and Ireland. But now being at Bristol, and finding Margaret Fell there, it opened to me from the Lord that the thing should be accomplished. After we had discussed the matter together, I told her ' if she also was satisfied with the accomplishing of it now, she should first send for her children,' which she did. When her daughters had come, I asked both them and her sons-in-law, ' if they had anything against it, or for it,' and they all severally expressed their satisfaction therein. Then I asked Margaret ' if she had fulfilled and performed her husband's will to her children.' She replied ' the children knew that.' Whereupon I asked them 'whether if their mother married, they should not lose by it.' And I asked Margaret 'whether she had done anything in lieu of it, which might answer to the children.' The children said 'she had answered it to them, and desired me to speak no more of it.' I told them 'I was plain and would have all things done plainly, for I sought not any outward advantage to myself.' So after I had acquainted the children with it, our intention of marriage was laid before Friends, both privately and publicly, to their full satisfaction, many of whom gave testimony thereunto that it was from God. Afterwards, a meeting being appointed for the accomplishing thereof in the meeting-house at Broadmead, in Bristol, we took each other, the Lord joining us together in honorable marriage, in the everlasting covenant and immortal Seed of Life. In the sense whereof living and weighty testimonies were borne thereunto by Friends, in the movings of the heavenly power which united us together. There was a certificate, relating both the proceedings and the marriage, openly read, and signed by the relations and by most of the ancient Friends of that city, besides many others from divers parts of the nation."

His singleness of purpose was shown in his refusing, under his own hand and seal, to have any part or benefit from his wife's estate, so careful was he to show that he sought no outward advantage, to the detriment of her children.

The honesty and uprightness of George Fox may be seen from this account, as well as his care to seek for direction in all the occurrences of life, temporal as well as spiritual. This principle of Divine guidance was the great rule of the faith and life of the early Friends; and the truth they felt called to proclaim as a fundamental doctrine of the gospel, that they who were adopted into the family of God through faith in His Son should be led by the Spirit of God.

But while receiving his wife as a gift from the Lord, the work to which our earnest evangelist felt called was not allowed to suffer thereby. After one week spent together in Bristol, they again separated; he to go on his Master's service and she to return to her old home, which now, by the provisions of Judge Fell's will, became the property of her daughters. It was not long before she was again thrown into prison on the old sentence of premunire. Her daughters applied in person to the King for her release, but she had many enemies who sought to retain her there, and it was not till after persistent and strenuous effort that a full discharge under the great seal, for herself and her estate, was obtained from King Charles.

As soon as George Fox had obtained this official document for his wife's release, he sent it to her with the request that he wished her to join him in London as soon as she could, because he had it on his mind from the Lord to proceed to America and the plantations in the West Indies, and that the vessel in which he intended to sail was then fitting out for her voyage.

The doctrines and tenets of the Society of Friends had been embraced not only in England, but also in the colonies of North America, where many meetings had been established. As there was now a cessation from persecution, and the disciplinary meetings for men and women had been organized, George Fox felt like visiting his brethren in the faith on the other side of the Atlantic Ocean. Twelve other ministers accompanied him, two of whom were women, and after attending the Yearly Meeting in London, which George Fox describes as a large and precious meeting, they bade farewell to their homes and sailed on the 12th of Sixth Month, 1671, in a large yacht, the Industry, bound for Barbadoes. This vessel was a fast sailer, but was in such a leaky state that the men were kept at the pumps day and night. Besides this cause for alarm, when they had been three weeks at sea they were chased by a Sallee man-of-war, a piratical vessel of the Algerine States. These pirates were in the habit of taking and plundering vessels and selling the passengers and seamen into slavery. The captain at first made light of the matter, assuring his passengers there was no danger, but as evening closed in the pirate gained rapidly upon them. The hearts of many on board the Industry were filled with fear lest they should fall into the hands of the pirates, but "the Friends were well satisfied in themselves, having faith in God and no fear upon their spirits." In this emergency the captain came to George Fox, for, said he, "if the mariners had taken Paul's advice they had not come to the damage they did." The answer was, "It is a trial of faith, and the Lord is to be waited on for counsel." The trusting servant shut himself up in his cabin, seeking direction from the Lord, "who showed me," he says, that "His life and power," was between them and the pursuing ship.

This he told to those on board, and advised the master of the vessel to follow his right course, nothing doubting. About eleven o'clock the watch shouted, " They are just upon us ! " which caused a commotion among the passengers. Even George Fox was on the point of going on deck, as, looking through the port hole of his cabin, he saw the pirate close by, but he remembered the promise of his Lord, that His power lay between them and the enemy, and quietly lay down again in his berth. At this critical moment, when they were about to be boarded by the pirate, the moon went down, a fresh breeze sprung up which carried them beyond his reach, and they saw him no more. The next morning being the first day of the week, at their usual meeting George Fox exhorted all present to remember " the mercies of the Lord who had delivered them, for they might all have been in the Turk's hands by that time, if the Lord had not saved them." Such is the tendency of the human heart to make light of God's mercies, that only one week passed before the captain tried to persuade the passengers that this was not a Turkish man-of-war, but a merchant ship going to the Canaries. Whereupon George Fox bade them beware of slighting the mercies of God.

When they reached the Barbadoes some time after, they heard in that port that a Sallee pirate had given chase to a monstrous yacht at sea, and when just upon the point of taking her, they lost her all at once, there being, as they described it, a spirit in her which they could not take. Well might George Fox say in his journal, " The Lord hid us."

The long and cruel imprisonments to which our friend had been subjected, and the many hardships he had endured, had left him in such a weak physical condition that he was ill all the voyage, which lasted seven weeks, and when they landed at Barbadoes was hardly able to walk. But he says, "I was pretty cheerful and my spirit kept above it all," and both at sea and before he could move about much on land his pen was busy in his Master's service.

The men's and women's meetings for discipline were held at the house of the Friend with whom he stayed, thus giving George Fox an opportunity for advising and counseling his brethren in the faith, in regard to their outward walk. His sympathies did not end here, but looking with paternal care over the colored race, he reminded Friends of their responsibility in regard to them. He exhorted them to "endeavor to train them up in the fear of God, that all might come to a knowledge of the Lord; that is, with Joshua, every master of a family might say, ' As for me and my house, we will serve the Lord.' " He also advised them to cause the overseers to deal mildly and gently with them, and after certain years of servitude they should be free.

Thus early in their acquaintance with the sin of slavery did Friends manifest an interest in the negro, which grew and strengthened as the extent of the evil was more fully realized. In 1727, at the Yearly Meeting of London, the following resolution was passed : " That the importing of negroes from their native country is not a commendable or allowable practice, and is therefore censured by this meeting."

During subsequent years minutes gradually increasing in strength were issued discountenancing slavery, till, in 1761, every one who persisted in the traffic was disowned from the Society of Friends.

In America the same gradual course may be noticed. In the early disciplines, directions were given that the slaves should be kindly treated, but before the beginning of this century, the Friends had by their official action renounced all participation in the guilt of slavery.

As George Fox regained his strength he held large meetings, which were attended by the leading men of the island, and were the means of dispersing some erroneous views which had prevailed in regard to Friends. At one of these meetings Colonel Lynn said, " Now I can gainsay such as I have heard speak evil of you, who say you do not own Christ, nor that He died, whereas I perceive you exalt Christ in all His offices, beyond what I have even heard before."

The faith of the early Friends in the Divinity of our Saviour was sometimes called in question, on account of the tenor of their preaching, in which they so frequently enforced attention to the leading of the Holy Spirit. But this was from no desire to undervalue the outward sacrifice for sin, nor the necessity of the blood which cleanseth. Many of them before they joined the Friends were persons highly esteemed for their piety, and while they zealously preached the doctrine of the new birth, they also felt there was danger in resting in a mere belief in what Christ had done and suffered for us, without pressing on to know Christ within, the hope of glory. They believed it was His blessed will to deliver from the power, as well as the guilt, of sin, and to enable those who do not frustrate His grace to walk before Him in newness of life. The religious world of that day was sadly deficient in the belief, while few ignored the outward sacrifice at Calvary, and thus the offices of the Holy Spirit, the Comforter, the Guide into all Truth, were the great themes of the ministry of the Friends.

In order to refute these slanderous reports, George Fox wrote a letter to the governor, in which the views of Friends were expressed in clear and forcible language. He declares their belief in the " everlasting God, the Creator of all things," in the Lord Jesus Christ, " the Redeemer and Saviour of the world," " the quickening Spirit, the second Adam, the Lord from Heaven, by whose blood we are cleansed, and our consciences sprinkled from dead works to serve the living God;" " in the Holy Scriptures which were given forth by the Holy Spirit through holy men of old," and are " profitable for doctrine, reproof, and instruction in righteousness."

After spending three months on the island of Barbadoes, and finding that he had performed all the service which his Master had for him there, he sailed for Jamaica, Eleventh Month, 8th, 1671, in company with four other Friends. Here he remained seven weeks, traveling up and down through the island, and his labors were so blessed that several new meetings were established there and the Friends greatly strengthened. He now wished to sail for the continent, and had his choice between two vessels, a frigate and yacht bound for the same port. The master of the frigate making what the Friends considered an unreasonable charge for their passage, they concluded to take the other. The two vessels sailed together, but the frigate, losing her way, fell into the hands of the Spaniards, by whom she was taken and plundered, and the master and mate made prisoners. On hearing of this the Friends rejoiced in their deliverance as fresh proof of the care of their covenant God.

Their voyage to the continent occupied seven weeks, and was full of difficulty and danger, owing to contrary winds. The following extract from the journal of this steadfast evangelist will show in whom his trust was placed: " The great God who is Lord of sea and land, and who rideth upon the wings of the wind, did by His power preserve us through many and great dangers, when by extreme stress of weather our vessel was many times likely to be upset and much of her tackling broken. And indeed we were sensible that the Lord was a God at hand, and that His ear was open to the supplication of his people. For when the waves were so strong and boisterous, and the storms and tempests so great that the sailors knew not what to do, but let the ship go which way she would, then did we pray to the Lord, who graciously heard us, calmed the winds and the seas, gave us seasonable weather, and made us rejoice in His salvation ; blessed be the holy name of the Lord, whose power hath dominion over all, whom the winds and seas obey."

The same thoughts were expressed by the poet Addison, and his concluding lines, though not uttered

by the lips of George Fox, were manifested in his
life.

    "In midst of dangers, fears, and death,
       Thy goodness I'll adore,
    And praise Thee for Thy mercies past,
       And humbly hope for more.

    "My life, if Thou preserv'st my life,
       Thy sacrifice shall be;
    And death, if death must be my doom,
       Shall join my soul to Thee."

The band of gospel laborers landed in Maryland,
just in time to attend a General Meeting which had
been appointed by John Burnyeat, an English Friend
who had been laboring in America for some time, and
was now about to return home. He was one of the
early converts of George Fox, and their encounter in
this strange land was so cheering, that John Burnyeat concluded to remain longer and assist his father
in the faith, in his service in this untried field. Many
of the prominent citizens of Maryland came to this
General Meeting, which lasted four days, and gave
great satisfaction. At the close of this public meeting more private ones were held among the Friends,
and George Fox had an opportunity of arranging
meetings for discipline, among both men and women.

The missionary band soon separated, going into
different districts, some to New England by sea, some
to Virginia, and George Fox, with John Burnyeat
and others, started for a journey by land to New
England, intending to stop and hold meetings by the
way. It was no slight undertaking to traverse those
inhospitable wilds, now teeming with the habitations and busy with the hum of men, and many

were the hardships they encountered. Sometimes
the journey was performed on horseback through
uninhabited forests; sometimes through treacherous
bogs; again they were obliged to pass over large riv-
ers exposed in open boats to the inclemency of the
season, and at times camped out for the night in
the snow, with no better shelter than the trunk of
an enormous tree. But no desire of ease or selfish
emolument had led this earnest worker to this land,
and he could say, " None of these things move me."

His labors were not confined to those of his own
faith, nor even to his own nation; but his sympathies extended to the native Indians, with whom he
had several interviews, and from whom he received
many acts of hospitality. At one time his course lay
through West Jersey, where there were no English
inhabitants, and the night overtook George Fox and
his friends in the woods. An Indian chief invited
them to his hut, spread mats for them to lie upon,
and shared with them the contents of his larder, very
scanty that day, as they had been unsuccessful in the
chase; thus adding another testimony to prove that
had the white man uniformly maintained a Christian
conduct toward his red brother, they might now be
bound together as friends, and the United States
would have been spared much expense of money, and
of that which is of far greater worth, the lives which
have been sacrificed in the attempts to subdue the
Indians.

Attending a half year's meeting at Oyster Bay on
Long Island, George Fox found occasion for the exercise of his sound judgment in dealing with some

Ranters who were very disturbing in the meetings of the Friends. " The Lord's power broke forth gloriously, and the glorious truth of God was exalted and set over all," and the messengers went on to Rhode Island, where the Yearly Meeting for all the Friends in New England was to be held. This meeting lasted six days, the first four being general gatherings for the public, which many of the inhabitants of the island attended, and manifested much attention. Two days more were occupied in men's and women's meetings for ordering the affairs of the church, in which the clear-headed veteran in the faith was of great use, after which followed a season which reminds one of the love feasts in the Apostolic days.

George Fox makes this entry in his journal: " When this great General Meeting in Rhode Island was ended, it was somewhat hard for Friends to part, for the glorious power of the Lord, which was over all, and His blessed truth and life flowing amongst them, had so knit and united them together, that they spent two days in taking leave one of another, and of the Friends on the island, and then being mightily filled with the presence and power of the Lord, they went away with joyful hearts to their various habitations."

The messengers dispersed again to their several fields of labor, George Fox holding and attending meetings on Rhode Island. His services were so satisfactory that in one place some of the leading men consulted together on the propriety of hiring him to be their minister. But self-emolument and self-exaltation had no place in this single-hearted man, and his comment is, "When I heard this, I said it was time for me to be gone, for if their eye was so much to me or any of us, they would not come to their own teacher. For this thing (hiring ministers) had spoiled many, by hindering them from improving their own talents, whereas our labor is to bring every one to his own teacher in himself."

After a stormy and tedious passage across Long Island Sound he came to Oyster Bay, and then to Flushing, where he held what he called "a glorious and heavenly meeting,"—many hundreds of people being there, some of whom came thirty miles to attend it.

This service performed, the laborers proceeded by sloop to the "New Country," now New Jersey, and landed at Middletown, where they took horses and rode to Shrewsbury. The road led through forests and over very bad bogs, one worse than all the rest, which the people called Purgatory, where they were obliged to let their horses slide down, the descent was so steep. At Shrewsbury a serious accident befell John Jay, one of the party. He was tying a horse, which started to run and threw the Friend on the ground, on his head. He was taken up as dead, and as his fellow companions stood around him mourning his loss and pitying his family, who were left in Barbadoes, George Fox says: "I took hold of his hair and his head turned any way, his neck was so limber. Whereupon I took his head in both my hands, and setting my knees against the tree I raised his head and perceived there was nothing broken. Then I put one hand under his chin and the other behind his head and raised his head two or three times with all my strength, and brought it in. I soon perceived his neck began to grow stiff again, and then he began to rattle in his throat and quickly after to breathe. The people were amazed, but I bid them have a good heart, be of good faith, and carry him to the house. They did so and set him near the fire. I bid them get him something warm to drink, and put him to bed. After he had been in the house a while he began to speak, but did not know where he had been. The next day we passed on, and he with us, sixteen miles to a meeting, through woods and bogs, and over a river where we swam our horses and went over ourselves on a hollow tree."

For nine days they traveled on through bogs and forests on their journey to Maryland, at times sheltered by the Indians at night, and preaching the word of the Lord to them, and sometimes bivouacking in the woods. At last, on the 18th of Seventh Month, they arrived weary and worn at the house of Robert Harwood, at Miles River. Hearing of a meeting next day they allowed themselves no time to rest, but went to attend it and then continued their journey four miles farther to another meeting, which the wife of a judge attended and declared she had rather hear the Friends once " than the priests a thousand times."

On the 3d of Eighth Month a General Meeting was held for all the Friends in Maryland. George Fox does not give the name of the place where it was held, but says it was near a river; " there were so many boats passing upon it that it was almost like the Thames." So many came that the house could not hold them, and one of the justices said " he had never seen so many people in that country before." The following record regarding it occurs in the journal : " It was a very heavenly meeting, wherein the presence of the Lord was gloriously manifested, and Friends were sweetly refreshed, the people generally satisfied, and many convinced ; for the blessed power of the Lord was over all ; everlasting praises to His holy name forever."

Three days were spent in public religious worship and two more in holding men's and women's meetings, particularly for the care and oversight of the Friends. It was the aim of George Fox, wherever he went, to encourage good order in the churches, and his efforts were greatly blessed.

Leaving, as he says, Friends well established in the Truth, George Fox and his associates went on towards Virginia, having several meetings on their way. The difficulties of the journey by no means vanished. At one time they were four days in an open rowboat, making what progress they could by day, and going on shore at night wet and weary with rowing, to find no house to receive them. Very little mention, however, is made of the privations of the journey, the blessed heavenly meetings which were held in different places overbalancing all the hardships. After a short stay in Virginia they visited North Carolina, holding meetings with the Friends, and also with the Indians. The following recommendation to the Friends of that region will show that George Fox fully realized the truth of the declaration that " in Christ Jesus there is neither Jew nor Gentile."

" And (it would be well) if you had sometimes meetings with the Indian kings and their people to preach the gospel of peace, of life, and of salvation to them. For the gospel is to be preached to every creature, and Christ hath tasted death for every man and died for their sins, that they might come out of death and sin, and live to Christ that died for them."

At the governor's house in Connie Oak Bay, in Virginia, he met a doctor who denied that the light or Spirit of God was given to every man, asserting that the Indians were destitute thereof. " Whereupon," says George Fox, " I called an Indian to us and asked him whether or not when he lied or did wrong to any one there was not something in him that reproved him for it." The Indian replied, " there was such a thing in him that did so reprove him and he was ashamed when he had done wrong or spoken wrong." The poor doctor, ashamed of being thus confounded before the governor, attempted to prove his position and at length went so far that he would not own the Scriptures. The governor, pleased with his guests, entertained them that night and next morning walked two miles through the woods with them, to show them the way.

After a tarriance of nearly two years in America, he says : " Having traveled through most parts of that country and visited most of the plantations, having sounded the alarm to all people where we came and proclaimed the day of God's salvation amongst them, we found our spirits began to be clear of these parts of the world and draw towards Old England again."

His last service in this country was attending a

general meeting of Friends in Maryland, which was a satisfactory parting interview. He set sail for England on the 21st of Third Month, 1673, but was detained by contrary winds so that ten days elapsed before they left the coast of Virginia. He records high winds and tempestuous weather on the remainder of their voyage; but it was performed in safety, and the missionary band had " many sweet and precious meetings " on board the vessel. On the 28th of Fourth Month they cast anchor in the harbor of King's Road, Bristol.

The account of the journey closes with this thanksgiving: " The great God who commands the winds, who is Lord of heaven, of earth and the seas, and whose wonders are seen in the deep, steered our course and preserved us from many imminent dangers. The same good hand of Providence that went with us, and carried us safely over, watched over us in our return and brought us safely back again; thanksgiving and praises be to His holy name forever."

CHAPTER XIII

WHILE George Fox was pursuing his evangelistic journey in America, his brethren at home were rejoicing in a temporary rest from persecution. In 1672, professing to be moved by the sufferings of a large portion of his subjects, and by a desire to promote union, the King issued a proclamation suspending "the execution of all penal laws against those who did not conform to the doctrine, discipline, and government of the church established by law."

Soon after the publication of this declaration of indulgence, Friends, ever on the alert to assist their brethren, hastened to take the necessary steps in regard to the four hundred sufferers who were incarcerated in prison, some of whom had been there ten or eleven years. George Whitehead and Thomas Moore were permitted to appear at the council chamber at Whitehall to represent their case. This they so successfully performed that the King said, " I will pardon them," and ordered the necessary letters patent to be made out. As the number of prisoners was so large, the fees for procuring their separate discharge would have amounted to a large sum, but the King ordered that the pardon, though including so many, should be charged but as one, and the Lord Keeper voluntarily remitted his fees. Eleven skins of parchment were requisite to make a fair copy of

7*

the document, and much labor was required, in order to render it available as quickly as possible to the weary ones so long separated from their homes and friends. The Friends in London, however, were not deterred by trouble or expense, and in a little time had the glad assurance that all who came within the scope of the letters patent were set at liberty.

There were other Dissenters in prison, and George Whitehead, the active agent of the Friends, was solicited to aid in their deliverance. This he cheerfully assented to, for he says, "Our being of different judgments and societies did not abate my charity or compassion, even towards them who had been my opposers in some cases. Blessed be the Lord my God, who is the Father and Fountain of mercies, whose love and mercies in Christ Jesus towards us should oblige us to be merciful and kind one to another."

He advised that the names of the prisoners should be sent to the King, with a petition for his warrant, to have them inserted in the same patent with the Quakers. The King granted the petition, and they also were set at liberty. Among the number thus released was John Bunyan, whose imprisonment in Bedford Jail for twelve years gave to the world the allegory which has been the means of helping many a Pilgrim in his journey from the City of Destruction.

The relief from persecution lasted only a short time, the jealousy of the English people being aroused by the favor shown to the Roman Catholics, and on the assembling of Parliament in 1673, the Commons, after a stormy debate, passed a resolution "that pe-

nal statutes in matters ecclesiastical cannot be suspended but by act of Parliament, and that an address
and petition for satisfaction should be presented to
the King." Charles was averse to the passage of
this resolution; but his purse was empty, and his
faithful subjects in the House of Commons made him
clearly understand that there would be no further
supplies till he agreed to their bill. He not only re-
called his declaration, but also assented to a bill to
check the growth of Popery, called the Test Act.
Thus the Friends were once more under the cruel
scourge of the infamous law of 1670, and the informers again hastened to their nefarious traffic.

George Fox, as we have learned, returned in safety
from his American tour, and on landing at Bristol
was joined by his wife and several other Friends.
They remained in that city some time, holding large
meetings, in which, as in other places, George Fox embraced the opportunity of calling the people to Christ
Jesus. In one of his sermons he thus points to Him:
" God was the first Teacher, and while man kept
under His teaching he was happy. The serpent was
the next teacher, and when man followed his teaching he fell into misery. Jesus Christ was the third
Teacher, of whom God said, 'This is my beloved
Son, in whom I am well pleased: hear ye Him;' and
who Himself said, 'Learn of Me.' Now Christ, who
said, 'Learn of Me,' and of whom the Father said,
'Hear ye Him,' said, 'I am the Way to God. I
am the Truth, I am the Life and the true Light.'
Therefore the Son of God is to be heard in all
things, who is the Saviour and Redeemer, who lay

down His life, and bought His sheep with His own blood."

Traveling through Gloucestershire and Wiltshire, he found occasion for wise and judicious treatment towards some who opposed the establishment of women's meetings. George Fox was, as we have seen, fully convinced that women, being heirs with the men of the same everlasting gospel of life and salvation, were consequently fitted to be helpmeets to men in the affairs of the church, as they are outwardly in civil and temporal matters. His enlightened views finally prevailed, and he says, " Women's meetings for that country were established in the blessed power of God." We next hear of him in London, laboring for the relief of the Friends who were suffering for refusing to close their shops on fast days and holidays. They considered such observances as mere human appointments, often accompanied with circumstances in which they could not conscientiously unite.

His labors were successful, and now this indefatigable worker turned his thoughts towards a little rest at Swarthmore. Although he had been married four years he had not yet been there, and, accompanied by his wife, two of her daughters, and Thomas Lower, her son-in-law, he turned his steps northward. His reasonable desire for a little rest was, however, thwarted by the malice of his enemies, who caused both T. Lower and himself to be arrested at the house of a Friend in Worcestershire. The charge against them was that they were holding large meetings to the prejudice of the Established Church.

They were committed to Worcester Jail, while Margaret Fox and her daughters proceeded to their home. The committal was entirely illegal, as the meeting had dispersed before the arrival of the justice at the house where it had been held, but in the case of Friends, their persecutors never scrupled to infringe the law, because there was always a sure snare in the administration of the oath, which the magistrates were empowered to tender on all occasions.

About a month after their seizure, they were brought before the Quarter Sessions, but nothing could be found against them. Justice Parker, however, was ready with the oath of allegiance, and upon the refusal of George Fox to take it he was remanded to prison. Thomas Lower was told he was at liberty, and on his querying why his father was not also released, the justices refused to say anything to him, and the court adjourned. After a time a writ of habeas corpus was obtained, and the case taken to the King's Bench at London. Thomas Lower was appointed by the sheriff his deputy to convey the prisoner to that city, where they arrived Twelfth Month, 2d, 1673. The next day George Fox appeared before the court, and the judges were disposed to release him, but Justice Parker, who had followed the prisoner to London, so prejudiced their minds that he was remanded to Worcester for trial. The only privilege allowed him was that he might go in his own time and way, provided he would be there at the Assize, which would begin in the second month. This gave an opportunity for attending the Yearly Meeting held in London, after which, by leisurely journeys, George Fox went back to Worcester. So great was the trust reposed in him, that his custodian on this journey was a boy of eleven years. At the Sessions the customary course was pursued; nothing was found against him; but the tendering of the oath insured imprisonment till the next sitting of the court. He was, however, left at liberty to come and go through the town as he pleased, which privilege he used in the service of his Master, reasoning with all he met, like the Apostle Paul, of "righteousness, temperance, and judgment to come." At one time, he says, a priest asked him if he was grown up to perfection. "I told him I was by the grace of God." Then he urged the words of John, "If we say that we have no sin, we deceive ourselves, and the truth is not in us," and asked, "what did I say to that?" "I said with the same Apostle, 'If we say that we have not sinned we make Him a liar, and His word is not in us,' who came to destroy sin and take away sin. So there is a time for people to see they have sinned, and there is a time for them to see they have sin, and there is a time for them to confess their sin and forsake it, and to know the blood of Christ to cleanse from all sin.'

After some further conversation, the priest said, "We must always be striving." George Fox, knowing the liberty wherewith Christ had made him free, said to his opponent: "It is a sad and comfortless sort of striving, to strive with a belief that we should never overcome." "I told him," he says in his journal, "that Paul, who cried out of the body of death, did also thank God who gave him the victory, through our Lord Jesus Christ. So there was a time of crying out for want of victory, and a time of praising God for the victory, and Paul said 'there is no condemnation to them that are in Christ Jesus.'" "Well, but," said the priest, "what say you to that Scripture, 'The justest man that is, sinneth seven times a day'?" "Why, truly," said George Fox, "there is no such Scripture," and his mouth was stopped.

While the Friends could not take an oath, they were loyal citizens and opposed to all plots and rebellions. This will be seen in a manifesto issued at this time by George Fox, addressed to the Judges of the King's Bench.

"This I do in truth and in the presence of God declare, that King Charles the Second is the lawful King of this realm, and of all other of his dominions; that he was brought in and set up King over this realm by the power of God; and I have nothing but love and good will to him and all his subjects, and desire his prosperity and eternal good. . . . . I do deny all plots and contrivances, and plotters and contrivers, against the King and his subjects, knowing them to be the works of darkness, the fruits of an evil spirit against the peace of the kingdom, and not from the Spirit of God, the fruit of which is love. I dare not take an oath, because it is forbidden by Christ and his Apostles; but if I break my Yea or Nay, let me suffer the same penalty as they that break their oaths.

(Signed) "GEORGE FOX."

In the Fifth Month, 1674, against the opinion of some of the judges, who discovered gross errors in his indictment, sentence of præmunire was pronounced upon him, and he was closely confined in Worcester Jail. His wife came from the north of England to be with him, and her services were greatly needed, as he was seized with a severe illness, from which his recovery seemed very doubtful. Every effort was made by his friends to obtain his release from prison, and at last his wife resolved to try the effect of a personal appeal to the King. She went up to London, and, obtaining an interview with King Charles, told him of the long and unjust imprisonment of her husband, and begged him, as by præmunire George Fox had become his prisoner, to release him from his bondage. Charles II. had kind words ready for her, but referred her to the Lord Keeper, who told her the King could only release him by a pardon. Secure in his innocence, George Fox refused the pardon, saying, " I had rather have lain in prison all my days, wherefore I chose to have the validity of my indictment tried before judges." His friends, however, succeeded in having him removed to London on a writ of habeas corpus, and Counsellor Corbet was employed to plead his cause. This gentleman astonished the judges by stating that it was illegal to imprison any one on a præmunire. This point established, the errors in the indictment were next considered, and were found to be so many and so gross, that the judges were united in the opinion that the prisoner should be released. Some of his adversaries would have again presented the oath of allegiance, saying George Fox was a dangerons man, and ought not to be at liberty; but Sir Matthew Hale replied, he had indeed heard some such reports, but he had heard many more good ones, and ordered George Fox freed by proclamation. Thus after an illegal imprisonment of fourteen months, he was honorably released, and Counsellor Corbet acquired great fame by his skillful management of the case.

The weary prisoner remained in London till after the Yearly Meeting of 1675, and then went by easy stages to Swarthmore, accompanied by his affectionate wife. The toils of his busy life, the rigor of his imprisonments, and the severe illness from which he was now recovering had left their traces on his robust frame, and rendered a season of rest necessary. For nearly two years he remained quietly at Swarthmore Hall, employing his respite from active service in collecting and arranging the various epistles he had written, and filing them away for future reference. As the time for the Yearly Meeting in 1676 drew near, he wrote a loving letter of counsel and advice, which was read at the meeting, as from an honored father in the church. Speaking to those who had known the Lord to be their Preserver in many a trying hour, he says: "Let every one's faith stand in the Lord's power, which is over all; through which they may be built upon the Rock, the Foundation of God, the Seed Jesus Christ. So all in Christ may be fresh and green, for He is the green tree that never withers. All are fresh and green that are grafted into and abide in Him, bringing forth heavenly, fresh fruits to the praise of God." Remembering that God is love and " he that dwelleth in love dwelleth in God," he thus exhorts : " And, friends, be tender to the tender principle of God in all. Shun vain disputes and janglings, both amongst yourselves and others, for that many times is like a blustering wind that hurts and bruises the tender buds and plants. Those disputers that were amongst the christians, about genealogies, circumcision, and the law, meats, drinks, and days, came to be the worst sort of disputers, whom the Apostle judged ; for such destroyed people from the faith. Therefore the Apostle exhorted the churches, that every one's faith should stand in the power of God, and to look to Jesus the author of it. There every graft stands in Christ, the Vine, quiet where no blustering storms can hurt them ; there is safety. There all are of one mind, one faith, one soul, one spirit, baptized into one body with the one Spirit, and made to drink into one Spirit, one church, one head, heavenly and spiritual, one faith in this head, Christ, who is the author of it, and hath the glory of it, one Lord to order all, who is the baptism into this one body." He closes his epistle with this beautiful exhortation : " Dwell in the love of God which passeth knowledge, and edifieth the living members of the body of Christ, which love of God come to be built up in, and in the holy faith. This love of God will bring you to bear all things, endure all things, and hope all things. From this love of God which you have in Christ Jesus, nothing will be able to separate you, neither powers nor principalities, heights nor depths, things present nor things to come, prisons nor spoiling of goods, neither death nor life. The love of

God keeps above all that which would separate from God, and makes you more than conquerors in Christ Jesus. Therefore in this love of God dwell, that with the same love you may love one another, and all the workmanship of God, that you may glorify God with your bodies, souls, and spirits, which are the Lord's. Amen."

Well would it have been for the church he loved so well, if his earnest, loving counsel had been attended to. In the two hundred years since this was written, there have been disputations about points analogous to the meats and drinks, and days and times, which disturbed the early Christians; disputes, too, carried on without the loving spirit he recommends, which have brought confusion into her borders, and crippled her usefulness.

In the early part of 1677, George Fox again felt the call to evangelistic labor, and leaving his quiet retirement at Swarthmore, he traveled by easy stages, as his health would permit, visiting meetings and strengthening the hands of his fellow believers. He reached London in time to attend the Yearly Meeting, which he describes as "a very glorious meeting, wherein the Lord's power was largely felt, and the affairs of truth sweetly carried on, in the unity of the Spirit, to the satisfaction and comfort of the upright-hearted; blessed be the Lord forever!" A new field of labor now opened before him, which he thus speaks of. "It was upon me from the Lord to go to Holland and preach the gospel there and in Germany." It will be interesting to pause for a moment to consider the state of religious feeling then existing in Holland.

The Separatists from the Established Church in England, finding no asylum in their own country, withdrew to Amsterdam about the year 1608, and joined themselves to the little company in that city who held similar views. Among these were such men as John Robinson, William Brewster, and William Bradford, to whom religious freedom was more than home and country. When the plan of colonizing America was proposed by the Virginia Company, and "such freedom as may stand with their liking" was promised, some of these same families who had emigrated to Holland, to find religious freedom, resolved to try the New World, and erect the standard of liberty of conscience on the rocky shores of Massachusetts. The farewell words of Pastor John Robinson to those who embarked in the Mayflower are in striking conformity to the testimony of George Fox, "I am nothing, Christ is all," and are worthy of remembrance. "I charge you before God and His blessed angels, that you follow me no further than you have seen me follow the Lord Jesus Christ. If God reveal anything to you by other instruments of His, be as ready to receive it as you were to receive any truth by my ministry; for I am verily persuaded, I am very confident, that God has more truth yet to break forth out of His holy Word. . . . . . I beseech you to remember, that you be ready to receive whatever truth shall be made known to you from the written Word of God." [1]

Well would it have been for the religious world, had this wise counsel been heeded; for, as has been

[1] *Inner Religious Life of Commonwealth.*

truly said, " the unwillingness of Christians to receive truth from unwelcome quarters has been a stumbling-block in every church."

Holland had been considered a missionary field before George Fox visited the country, and a little company of Friends had been gathered there, and in other parts of the United Provinces, through the labors of William Caton and others. But while this country was distinguished for abstaining from enacting laws designed to interfere with the right of liberty of conscience, the magistrates sometimes connived at the infliction of abuse of innocent persons, and Friends were exposed here, as in England, to persecution. In East Friesland the following petition was presented to the court: " Whereas, the wicked sect of the Quakers are found in these United Provinces, and also sprung up here in East Friesland, you are desired to watch against it in time, that that devilish error might not creep in further." It was found, however, that banishment and other punishments inflicted on such honest, industrious men as the Friends diminished the trade of the cities, and the authorities wisely determined to retain this class of citizens, by allowing freedom in worshiping God.

On the 25th of Fifth Month, 1677, George Fox set sail for Holland, accompanied by William Penn, Robert Barclay, and others, and arrived at Rotterdam on the 28th. After holding some meetings they passed on to Amsterdam, to attend the Quarterly Meeting, which was held at the house of Gertrude Dirick Nieson. After this meeting George Fox called the

Friends together and arranged for "a Monthly, Quarterly, and Yearly Meeting, to be held at Amsterdam, for Friends in the United Provinces of Holland, and in Embden, the Palatinate, Hamburg, Frederickstadt, Dantzic, and other places in and about Germany."

In obedience to the command of the Holy Spirit, the missionary band separated soon after their arrival in Holland, each going to the work to which he felt called of the Lord. As a wise legislator, a portion of the work devolving upon George Fox was to build up the little communities and establish men's and women's meetings for discipline, thus bringing the Society into a similar organization with that of Great Britain and America. He also held large meetings, which were attended by persons of various denominations, in which, he says, "I declared the everlasting gospel." This met with a response on the part of the hearers, and at Harlem and Harlingen the minister rose after George Fox had finished, saying, "I pray God to prosper and confirm this doctrine, for it is truth, and I have nothing against it." Not only in the gathered assemblies did George Fox witness for his Lord, but he was always on the alert to embrace the opportunities presenting before him. "Many times," he says, "in mornings, and at noons and nights, at the inns and on the ways, as I traveled, I spake to the people, warning them of the day of the Lord." His pen was also busily employed in his Master's service. A little synopsis of his writings will show his catholic spirit, and also how much interest he felt in the welfare of his people. Hearing Friends

were suffering from persecution at Dantzic, he wrote
a loving letter to them, encouraging them to be faithful. Another letter of warning was sent to the magistrates of Oldenburg and Hamburg, telling them of
the " great and terrible judgments of the day of the
Lord God Almighty." The ambassadors of the King
of France, of the United Provinces, and of several
other rulers of Europe met at this time in the city of
Nimeguen, to consult about the peace of christendom.
This was a subject dear to the heart of this peace-lov-
ing christian, and he addressed an epistle to them,
beseeching them, " as ye love God and Christ and
christianity and its peace, make peace, so far as ye
have power, among christians, that you may have the
blessing." Before the year ended a peace was concluded.

He also wrote a loving letter of advice to the Princess Elizabeth of the Rhine, niece of Charles I.
She was a sweet, humble christian, and governed her
little principality with judgment and kindness. William Penn and Robert Barclay visited her, and had
religious meetings in her palace, much to her satisfaction. At parting she said to them, " Let me desire
you to remember me, though I live at so great a distance, and you should never see me more. I thank
you for this good time. Be assured, though my condition subjects me to divers temptations, yet my soul
has strong desires after the best things." The princess responded to the letter of George Fox in the following terms : " I cannot but have a tender love to
those that love the Lord Jesus Christ, and to whom
it is given not only to believe on Him, but also to suf-

fer for Him ; therefore your letter and your friends' visit have been both very welcome to me. I shall follow their and your counsel, as far as God will afford me light and unction, remaining still your loving friend."

The respect the princess held for Friends prompted her to influence the English court in their favor, and more than once she endeavored to preserve them from the penalties of the laws against conventicles. She died at the age of sixty, much esteemed and beloved.

Galenus Abrahams, a Mennonite teacher, sought a conference with the Friends, asserting that no one in the present day could be accepted as a messenger of God unless he confirmed his doctrines by miracles. William Penn, George Keith, and George Fox accepted the challenge, and a long dispute followed, in which, George Fox says, " The Baptist was much confounded, and the truth gained ground." The arguments are not given ; but if, as was usually the case, Friends used the Bible to support their position, they would silence him, for John the Baptist was surely a messenger of the Lord, and yet we are told he " did no miracles." Galenus Abrahams was not convinced, but on the second visit of George Fox to Holland, the two opponents met in a friendly manner, and Galenus " confessed in some measure to the truth."

In the autumn of 1667, this earnest evangelist returned to England, and was most gladly welcomed by his brethren, a thousand people flocking to his first meeting at Harwich. He reached London on the

9th of Ninth Month, and on the First Day following attended Gracechurch Street meeting, where his
record is : " The Lord visited us with His refreshing
presence, and the glory of the Lord surrounded the
meeting.   Praised be the Lord."

8

WE have now approached an era in the life of George Fox when he was exposed to a new trial. Persecution from without had long been familiar to him ; but now a keener thorn pierced his soul, in the internal dissensions of his loved Society. To understand the position of the Friends at this time, it will be necessary to refer to some of the earlier sects, whose tenets had in some measure influenced Fox and his coadjutors in founding the Society of Friends.

In the reign of Elizabeth, there were a large number who felt constrained to dissent from many of the ceremonies of the Established Church, and who sought a more simple faith and a mode of worship more consonant with the Apostolic rule, " that all may prophesy one by one, — that all may learn and all may be comforted." This freedom was not, however, in accordance with the Queen's views, and two of a congregation of thirty who assembled at a private house for worship were burned to death by her order.

The longing for truth could not, however, be burned out of the hearts of many in England, and one sect rose after another, each differing somewhat, but united in the desire that the church should be separated from the state, and only bound to submit to the order " which Christ her Lord and King had instituted." To obtain this freedom many, as we have seen, fled to Holland and America ; but many remained in England, suffering cruel persecution, and even laying down their lives for the sake of the Truth.

Two of these sects, the Seekers and Ranters, have often been confounded with Friends, and deserve particular notice. Cromwell said : " To be a Seeker is to be of the next best sect to a Finder," and in the days when men's hearts were so stirred within them, there was an earnest craving for something more than an external show of religion. The Seekers, as their name implies, were looking for a revival of the Apostolic days, — for more purity in religion. They could have no church fellowship because they could not find in any of the churches the New Testament pattern. They waited, in this time of apostasy, for an apostle, or angel mighty in the Spirit, to give some visible manifestation of their being sent of the Lord.

The Ranters, on the contrary, held views in the opposite extreme. They maintained they had found God, and that by His Spirit He dwelt in them. They needed not the Scripture, for they were taught by the Spirit, which inspired them. They were no longer to mind Christ who died at Jerusalem, but to mind Christ in themselves. William Penn says : " This people obtained the name of Ranters, from their extravagant courses and practices. They interpreted Christ's fulfilling the law for us to be a discharging us from any obligation and duty the law required, instead of the condemnation of the law for sins past, upon faith and repentance ; and that now it was no sin to do that which before it was a sin to commit, —

the slavish fear of the law being taken off by Christ, — and now all things were good that a man did, if he did but do them with the mind and persuasion that they were so."

The Society of Friends, and the clear definite views they professed, were equally opposed to the quietism of the one sect and the ranterism of the other. They told the Seekers they had found what the others were so vainly waiting for, declaring that the kingdom of God consists not in groaning for adoption, but in "righteousness and peace and joy in the Holy Ghost." To the Ranters they said : " We dearly and truly own the Holy Scriptures, given by inspiration, as a true and infallible testimony of Christ, spoken forth by the Holy Spirit, which is our Guide, Teacher, and Leader, and these are written for our learning."

Many of these two sects joined the Friends, and the influence of their previous views we shall now see affecting the Society and causing disunity and dissatisfaction with Fox and his coadjutors.

Mention has already been made of the opposition, manifested in some places, to the establishment of meetings for discipline. This, some urged, restricted the freedom into which we are called by the gospel ; and these desired that every one should be left to regulate his course by the Light of Christ in himself, without being amenable to others. The discipline was denounced as an encroachment on the right of private judgment, similar to that practiced by the church of Rome, and George Fox, the instrument by which these meetings were set up, received loud and unsparing invective as seeking to lord it over " God's heritage."

In a pamphlet written as early as 1663, the beginning of this movement might be seen. In it the writer
urges that no one shall be obliged to "act outwardly"
further than he "saw inwardly." The regular assembly for public worship was to be superseded by
the more spiritual gathering, as each one felt impelled.
The meeting-house was only to be used when Friends
"felt the stirrings of life," with respect to both time
and place. There had been enough of earnest evangelistic effort; the time had come for Friends to sit
under their own vine and fig-tree, and enjoy the fruit
of their previous labor.

These views, of course, struck at the root of all
order, and their indulgence would soon lead to anarchy
and confusion. The smouldering embers broke out
afresh in 1673, and there were very few of the prominent Friends who were not drawn into the controversy. The assumption of the right of private judgment, whether opposed or not to the letter and spirit
of the New Testament as understood by the church,
the disregard of outward rules, and the opposition to
instrumental teaching were some of the points in
question. The efforts of George Fox to establish a
system of church government were denounced as if
from selfish motives, to increase his own influence.
His care that all the meetings should be supplied
with a teaching ministry was considered subversive.
of that dependence upon the leading of the Holy
Spirit which would move the ministers to go whither
the Lord willed.

The question of the use of singing in worship was
another subject of difference. The early Friends,

in common with some other Dissenters, objected to
the custom " of the singing, by a mixed multitude,
of all description of Psalms," but had no controversy
with those " who live and dwell in the grace of God,
and sing with grace in the heart." When George
Fox was appealed to on this question, as he was upon
all points of church government, he says, in 1673,
" Why should not them as sings have liberty of conscience to sing in your meetings? I do look upon
thee as a competent judge whether they sing in grace
or no." [1] In 1675, the Yearly Meeting issued this
advice " concerning sighing, groaning, or singing in
the church :" " It hath been, and is, our loving sense
and constant testimony, according to our experience
of the divers operation of the Spirit and power of
God in His church, that there has been, and still is,
serious sighing, sensible groaning, and reverent singing, breathing forth a heavenly sound of joy, with
grace in the Spirit and understanding, and which is
not to be quenched or discouraged in any, unless im-
moderate."

On the other hand, it was maintained that " singing, or speaking singingly in prayer, preaching, or
with a vocal voice, was an abomination." Thus, as has
often been done since, while pleading for liberty to follow what they believed to be right, the opponents of
Fox and his friends laid down stringent rules for others, and limited the action of the Holy Spirit to the
channel in which they themselves were wont to move.

The power of the Yearly Meeting of London was
very obnoxious to those who questioned " whether

[1] *Inner Religious Life of Commonwealth.*

the judgment of any one part of the members of
Christ's body could become a bond upon any other
part of the said body, further than their understandings were illuminated." It would not be desirable to
question the minor points of difference, as, when all
order is denounced, the means for maintaining that
order also fall under condemnation. It must be admitted that these dissatisfied ones took, as George
Fox says, more pains to unsettle and disquiet the
church than they had ever taken for the cause of
truth. Disputes in those days of controversy were
carried on with great warmth, and the brunt of op-
probrium fell upon George Fox as the exponent of
liberal views.

Amid all the abuse and misapprehension the christian character of the champion for truth shone out
brighter and brighter. Seeking to be clothed with
the meekness and gentleness of Christ, he returned
not railing for railing, but tried to convince the dis-
affected of their error, and induce them to remain
with their brethren. His efforts, however, were unavailing. In Westmoreland, two ministers, named
John Story and John Wilkinson, who had been earnest laborers for the Lord, left the Friends, and, gathering around them a company similarly affected with
themselves, established a separate meeting at Preston
in 1675. This example was followed in London,
Wiltshire, Bristol, and other parts of Westmoreland,
causing great pain to George Fox. Various efforts
were made to reconcile the differences. A meeting
was arranged between Story, Wilkinson, and Rodgers,
on the part of the Separatists, and George Fox and

others sympathizing with him. This was held at Drawel near Sedburgh, Second Month, 3d, 1676. Four days were spent in endeavoring to convince the Separatists that there will be unity of action in the church as each individual is led by the Holy Spirit, for God is a God of order, and His Spirit can never prompt to disorder or confusion. George Fox gives the following account of this meeting : " Most of their arrows were shot at me ; but the Lord was with me, and gave me strength in his power to cast back their darts of envy and falsehood upon themselves. Their objections were answered, and things were opened to the people ; a good opportunity it was, and service-able to the truth, for many that before were weak were now strengthened and confirmed ; some that were doubting and wavering were satisfied and set-tled, and faithful Friends were refreshed and com-forted in the springings of life."

The christian spirit manifested in this gathering affected Wilkinson and Story, and soon after they signed a paper declaring they had " no wish to op-pose any faithful brethren in the practice of those things they believe are their duty." Several of their followers were received back into the Society on con-fession of the error into which they had been drawn. The separate meetings became very small, and by the year 1709 the Separatists were reported to have be-come very few in number. Any one, however, who carefully examines the history of this Society in the eighteenth century, will see the influence of their views operating disadvantageously to the healthy growth of the church founded by George Fox and his coadjutors.

But we must turn from these intestine dissensions to the contemplation of the condition of England in the year 1678 ; Charles II. being the reigning monarch. The popular mind was in a state of tumult. Faint whispers and undefined suspicions of some evil were followed by the discovery of what was declared to be "a damnable plot, contrived and carried on by Popish recusants, against the life of the King and the Protestant religion." Titus Oates, a degraded clergyman of the English Church, appeared before Parliament, and made astounding revelations, implicating some high in office, of complicity with the Pope and Jesuits in a plot to subvert the religion of England.

Although the informer varied his statements before the different parties who heard him, he was declared to be the "Saver of the Nation," and had a pension of £1200 a year granted him. The trade of a Protestant witness proving so profitable, others came forward to reap part of the gain, among them William Bedloe, a convicted thief and swindler, who had just been liberated from Newgate. Notwithstanding the character of the informers, their statements were eagerly believed ; the terror excited by the plot aroused the public mind to such a degree that " reason could no more be heard than a whisper in a hurricane." Nothing but blood could satisfy the people, and to be accused was, almost in every case, to be condemned to death. The House of Commons passed a bill, which reached the third reading in the House of Lords, excluding all Papists from sitting in either house. The Duke of York protested warmly against this bill, which would disqualify him from the succession, and it was amended by a proviso that this did not affect him. The King dissolved Parliament after a session of eighteen years, and for the next few years alternately prorogued and dissolved it, finding it too much inclined to assert its rights, yet needing the subsidies he obtained from it.

The Friends took no part in these political turmoils, which were the occasion of much suffering to them, for all parties seemed to unite on the common ground of persecuting the Quakers. They were accused by some of being Popish recusants, and this enlisted the prejudices of the people against them, while others declared if they were not Papists they were plotters against the government.

In order to prevent the effect of these calumnious reports, George Fox wrote the following declaration, addressed to the new Parliament : " It is our principle and testimony to deny and renounce all plots and plotters against the King, or any of his subjects ; for we have the Spirit of Christ, by which we have the mind of Christ, who came to save men's lives and not to destroy them ; and we would have the King and all his subjects to be safe. Wherefore we do declare that we will endeavor to our power to save and defend him and them, by discovering all plots and plotters, which shall come to our knowledge, that would destroy the King or his subjects ; this we do sincerely offer to you. But as to swearing and fighting, which in tenderness of conscience we cannot do, ye know that we have suffered these many years for our conscientious refusal thereof. And now that the Lord hath brought you together, we desire you to relieve us, and free us from these sufferings, and that ye will not put upon us to do those things which we have suffered so much and so long already for not doing, for if you do ye will make our bonds stronger, instead of relieving us."

In 1680 a paper was presented to the King and Parliament, giving an account of the sufferings Friends had undergone since the Restoration. Ten thousand had been imprisoned, two hundred and forty-three had died in prison, while the loss of property to which they had been subjected from their prosecution as Papish recusants had indéed been grievous. William Penn and others went before a committee of the House, and clearly demonstrated the truth of these statements, and Sir Christopher Musgrave, a zealous Churchman, expressed his disgust at the treatment Friends had received, saying the prisons were full of them, many of them had been excommunicated for small matters, and that it was a shame and a scandal for the church to use the Quakers so hardly on every trivial occasion. Both Houses finally passed a bill exempting Protestant dissenters from the penalties imposed by the Acts of Elizabeth, but when it was to be presented to the King for his signature it could not be found. It was said that it had been secreted by order of Charles II.

During 1683 and 1684 the fire of persecution blazed fiercely, yet the Friends continued almost universally faithful to their principles. An epistle addressed by George Fox to those remaining steadfast shows the care among the early Friends to be honest in their dealings. He exhorts them to remember the

care that existed among them, that no man should
suffer by them. When they bought goods on credit
he exhorted them to tell their creditors the danger
there was that everything might be taken from them,
and when fines were imposed, to be careful to use
their own property, to offer that which was their own,
that no man should suffer by them. This, he says,
" wrought a very good savor in the hearts of many
people, seeing such a righteous, just, and honest principle in Friends." He desires them to continue this
practice, that thus their light may shine even in suffering.

CHAPTER XV.

THE continued and severe persecution of the Friends, in the latter part of the reign of Charles II., rendered the presence of George Fox at London almost indispensable. He could not rest in his pleasant home at Swarthmore while his brethren were in danger, and accordingly left it in the early part of 1680, and never returned there again. " It being a suffering time with Friends," he says, " I had not freedom to be long from the city."

His labor was very varied; sometimes visiting Friends " in prison for the testimony of Jesus," encouraging them in their sufferings, and exhorting them to stand faithful to the testimony the Lord had committed to them to bear, and sometimes visiting those who were sick and weak in body, or troubled in mind, helping to bear up their spirits from sinking under their infirmities.

A determined effort was now being made to suppress the meetings of Friends. In London and in some of the adjoining towns armed men were stationed at the different meeting-houses, and constables frequently attended with warrants to arrest the speakers. Yet in George Fox's journal allusion is frequently made to glorious and blessed meetings, in which the power of the Lord controlled the will of man, and the soldiers went away without making any disturbance.

It could not be expected that an old veteran like George Fox, who had long been in the fore-front of the battle, should keep away from these scenes of conflict. Accordingly entries like the following are frequently found in his journal: " At one time I intended to go a mile or two out of town, to visit a Friend who was not well, but hearing that the King had sent to the mayor to put the laws in execution against Dissenters, and that the magistrates intended to nail up the meeting-house doors, I had not freedom to go out of town, but was moved to go to the meeting in Gracechurch Street, and, notwithstanding all threats, a great meeting it was, and very quiet ; the glory of the Lord shone over all."

The time for the Yearly Meeting now approached, and those who came up to London from the country meetings to attend it did so at the risk of their liberty. There were many who were ready to inform against them and denounce their meetings as prejudicial to the safety of the realm, but notwithstanding the danger the attendance at the meeting was large. George Fox thus speaks of the occasion : " The Lord was with us, His power preserved us and gave us a sweet, a blessed opportunity to wait upon Him, to be refreshed together with Him, and to perform His service for His truth and people." Soon after the Yearly Meeting he wrote a beautiful epistle, which must have fallen like dew upon his sorely tried but steadfast brethren. The following is an extract.

" DEAR FRIENDS, — My love is to you all in the holy Seed that reigns over all. And my desire is, that every one, both male and female, may feel the Seed of Christ in you, which is heir of the promise of life eternal, that ye may all grow up in Christ Jesus your head, and be built upon Him, the rock and foundation that God hath laid, which stands sure over all rocks and foundations in the world ; that ye may eat and drink of this spiritual rock, the spiritual water and food ; so that ye may truly and inwardly say, that your rock and foundation, your bread and water of life, is from heaven, and your bread and water is sure ; and that ye know His voice that feeds you, and leads into the pastures of life, which are always fresh and green. In this your affections are set upon things that are above, seeking that which comes down from above, where Christ sits at the right hand of God, making intercession for you ; who is your Mediator, making peace between God and you ; who is your heavenly Bishop, to oversee you, that ye keep in His light, life, and power, and do not go astray from His heavenly fold and pasture, that He, your Shepherd, may feed you therein ; who is your Prophet, to open to you the fulfilling of the promise and prophesies, Himself being the substance ; that ye may live in Him, and He in you, yea, and reign in your hearts, there to exercise His offices, His pro-phetical, priestly, and kingly office, who is heavenly and spiritual."

The advice in the following letter, written in the same year, is applicable to the church to-day, and may well claim her attention.

"FRIENDS AND BRETHREN, — Who have received the peaceable truth, let the fruits of its peaceableness and of your quiet spirit appear in all your meetings, and in all your words and actions; for He that inhabits eternity dwells with an humble heart, He gives grace to the humble and resisteth the proud. Heaven is His throne, and the earth ye walk upon is His footstool; happy are ye that see and know Him that is invisible.

"And now, Friends, let all things be done in your meetings, and otherwise, in love, without strife or vain-glory, for love fulfills the law, love overcomes and edifies the body of Christ; there is neither self nor envy in love, neither is it puffed up, but abides and bears all things. See that this love of God have the sway in you all and over you all. Christ saith, ' Blessed are the poor in spirit, for theirs is the kingdom of heaven. Blessed are they that mourn, for they shall be comforted. Blessed are the meek, for they shall inherit the earth. Blessed are they that do hunger and thirst after righteousness, for they shall be filled. Blessed are the merciful, for they shall obtain mercy. Blessed are the pure in heart, for they shall see God. Blessed are the peacemakers, for they shall be called the children of God. Blessed are they that are persecuted for righteousness' sake, for theirs is the kingdom of heaven. Blessed are ye, when men shall revile you, and persecute you, and shall say all manner of evil against you falsely, for my sake. Rejoice and be exceeding glad, for great is your reward in heaven; for so persecuted they the prophets that were before you.'

" Now, Friends, here is a great deal in these words; and all must be in these states and conditions if they have those blessings. The children of God are peacemakers, and strive to make peace in the truth ; and to live in peace with all men if it be possible. So live in peace and good will to all men ; which good will is both for their sanctification and salvation. And, Friends, consider the wisdom of God, which is from above, is pure, peaceable, gentle, and easy to be entreated, full of mercy and good fruits, without partiality and without hypocrisy. Dear Friends, let this pure, peaceable, gentle wisdom that is from above, that is easy to be entreated, and is full of mercy and good fruits, be exercised and practiced in all the true churches of Christ, so that wisdom may be justified of her children. For the works of the flesh or fleshly spirit are hatred, variance, wrath, strife, envyings, drunkenness, revelings, adultery, fornications, lasciviousness, uncleanness, etc., and they which do such things shall not inherit the kingdom of God. But the fruits of the Spirit of God are love, joy, peace, long-suffering, gentleness, goodness, faith, meekness, temperance. So, dear Friends and brethren, strive to exceed one another, and all people upon the earth, in humility, meekness, gentleness, temperance, love, patience, pureness, and in mercy ; then ye will show forth the fruits of the Spirit of God, and of His heavenly wisdom that is from above. In this, wisdom will be justified of her children, ye will be the salt of the earth, the light of the world set on a hill, that cannot be hid; and your moderation will appear to all men. Be ye just and righteous, faithful and true in all your words, dealings, and conversations, so that ye may answer the truth in all people; for Christ saith, His Father is glorified by such as bring forth fruits when men do see their good works; for he that doeth righteousness is accepted with God. And he that dwells in love dwells in God; for love is His habitation. Let that be the habitation of every one that hath received the truth; for if it be not, such do not dwell in God, let them profess what they will. Therefore my desire is, that all you who have received Christ the Seed, which bruises the serpent's head, may walk in Him, your sanctuary, life, and salvation, your rest and peace. Amen.   G. F.

" LONDON, *the 14th of the Sixth Month,* 1683."

The following earnest appeal to the servants of the Lord is worthy of serious attention, remembering the command, " Occupy till I come."

" FRIENDS, — Dwell in the Living Spirit, and quench not the motions of it in yourselves, nor the movings of it in others; though many have run out and gone beyond their measures, yet many more have quenched the measure of the Spirit of God, and have become dead and dull, and have questioned through a false fear; so there hath been hurt both ways. Therefore be obedient to the power of the Lord and His Spirit; war with that Philistine that would stop up your wells and your springs. And the belief in the power keeps the spring open and none to despise prophecy, neither to quench the Spirit; so that all may be kept open to the spring, that every one's cup may run over. For you may all prophesy one by one, and the spirit of the prophets is subject to the prophets ; would all the Lord's people were prophets, said Moses in his time, when some found fault : but the last time is the christian's time ; who enjoys the substance, Christ Jesus, and His church is called a royal priesthood, offering up spiritual sacrifices ; and His church are His believers in the light. And so in the light every one should have something to offer ; and to offer an offering in righteousness to the living God, else they are not priests ; and such as quench the Spirit cannot offer, but become dull. I will pour out of my Spirit upon all flesh in the last time, saith the Lord, which is the true christian's time : God's sons and daughters shall prophesy, and your young men shall see visions, and old men shall dream dreams ; and on my servants and handmaids I will pour out of my Spirit in those days, and they shall prophesy. Now, Friends, if this be fulfilled, servants, handmaids, sons, daughters, old men, young men, every one is to feel the Spirit of God, by which you may see the things of God and declare them to His praise ; for with the heart man doth believe, and with the mouth confession is made unto salvation ; first he has it in his heart, before it comes out of his mouth ; and this is beyond that brain-beaten heady stuff which man has long studied, about the saints' words which the holy men of God spake forth, as they were moved of the Holy Ghost.

" So with the Holy Ghost, and with the light and power of God, do you build upon Christ, the Foundation and Life ; and by the same heavenly Light, and Power, and Spirit do you labor in the vineyard, and do you minister and speak forth the things of God, and do you dig for your pearls; therefore bring them forth, and let them be seen how they glister. Friends, you see how men and women can speak enough for the world, for merchandise, for husbandry, the plowman for his plow; but when they should come to speak for God they quench the Spirit, and do not obey God's will.

" But come, let us see what the wise merchants can say: have they found the pearl and field, and purchased the field which yields those glorious glistering pearls? Let us see, what can you say for God, and that heavenly merchandise? What can the plowman say for God with his spiritual plow? — is the fallow ground plowed up? has he abundance of the heavenly seed of life? So what can the heavenly husbandman say? — has he abundance of spiritual fruit in store? What can the thresher say? — has he gotten the wheat out of the sheaf, the heavenly wheat, with his heavenly flail? And let us see, what can the spiritual plowman, husbandman, and thresher say for God; and how they have labored in the vineyard, that they may have their penny. Some are breakers of clods in the vineyard, some are weeders, some are cutting off the brambles and bushes, and fitting the ground, and cutting up the roots with the heavenly axe for the seed; some are harrowing in, some are gathering and laying up the riches. So, you may see, here are merchants, plowmen, harrowers, weeders, reapers, and threshers in God's vineyard, yet no one is to find fault with another, but all laboring in their places, praising the Lord, looking to Him for their wages, their heavenly penny of life, from the Lord of life.

" So none are to quench the Spirit, nor to despise prophecy, lest ye limit the Holy One ; and every one is to minister as he hath received the grace, which hath appeared to all men, which brings salvation ; so that the Lord's grace, His light, and truth, and Spirit, and power, may have the passage and the rule in all men and women ; that by it and from it in all, He may have the glory, who is blessed forever and forever. The Lord hath said: 'From the rising of the sun to the going down of the same, my name shall be great among the Gentiles.' Now mark, Friends, this is a large space, wherein God's name shall be great ; and the Lord further saith : ' In every place incense shall be offered unto my name, and a pure offering ; for my name shall be great among the heathen, saith the Lord of hosts.' Now mark, Friends, this heavenly incense and pure offering is a spiritual offering, which is to be offered by the Spirit to God, who is a Spirit ; then here none quenches the Spirit of God in his own heart ; and all such come under the title of the royal priesthood, offering up spiritual sacrifices ; which royal priesthood has a Priest that lives forever, Christ Jesus.

" And, Friends, do not quench the Spirit, nor abuse the power ; when it moves and stirs in you, be obedient ; but do not go beyond, nor add to it, nor take from it ; for if you do, you are reproved, either for going beyond, or taking from it. And when any have spoken forth the things of the Lord, by His power and Spirit, let them keep in the power and

Spirit that keeps them in the humility, that when they have spoken forth the things of God, they are neither higher nor lower, but still keep in the power, before and after; and being obedient to the Spirit and power of God, it keeps them from deadness, and alive to God, and keeps them in a sense that they do not go beyond and run out, as some you know have done: and all that hath come for want of living in the power of God, and in His Spirit, which keeps all things in subjection and in order, and in the true fear of the Lord, always to feel the presence of the Lord with you.

"Come, fishermen, what have you caught with your nets? What can you say for God? Your brethren, Peter and John, fishermen, could say much for God. Read in the Acts and you may see; I would not have you degenerate from their spirits.

"Shepherds and herdsmen, where are you? What can you say now for God, whose abiding is much in the fields? David, Jacob, and Amos, your fellow-shepherds and herdsmen (do not you see?), they could say much for God; I would have you to be like them, and not to degenerate from their spirit.

"Come, tradesmen, tent-makers, physicians, and custom-men, what can you say for God? Do not you read that your fellow-tradesmen in ages past could say much for God? Do not degenerate from their spirit. Do not you remember the accusations of the wise and learned Grecians, when the apostles preached Christ among them, that they were called poor tradesmen and fishermen? Therefore be faithful. The preachers of Jesus Christ now are the same to the wise of the world as then. G. F."

In the Third Month, 1684, a little missionary band started for Holland, to see how it fared with their brethren ; and among this number we find George Fox.

They attended the Yearly Meeting held at Amsterdam, and traveled about the country for six weeks, visiting the different meetings. This was the last journey George Fox was able to take, and on his return was so feeble that he was obliged to remain at the house of his son-in-law, William Meads, at Kinston, for some time, reaching London in the autumn of the same year.

" After returning from his last visit to Holland George Fox did not travel far from London, his usual residence during the latter part of his life. His health had been gradually declining for some years, in consequence of his many and grievous imprisonments, and the great fatigue of body and mind occasioned by his long travels for the promotion of the cause of truth, and by his incessant labors in ' defense of the gospel' against the clamor and opposition of apostate brethren, and the unfounded imputations of others, decidedly hostile to the truth as it is in Jesus. His solicitude, however, to promote the welfare of the Society, and procure relief to his friends under suffering, both at home and abroad, remained undiminished. In the course of his declining state he wrote many epistles to his friends, some of sympathy and consolation, to encourage and strengthen them in their deep sufferings ; others of counsel, exhortation, and reproof, ' stirring up the pure mind by way of remembrance,' and laboring to build them up in the most holy faith; and on all occasions seeking not his own honor, but the honor of God only, and the edification of his church and people.

"Besides these epistles he wrote also others of a more extended character. There are three addressed to the Jews; and papers in behalf of the doctrine of the gospel, and against persecution, to be delivered to the following rulers: the Great Turk, the magistrates of Malta, the Emperor of Austria, the Kings of France and Spain, the Pope, and the Emperor of China. And in 1688, Sultan Mahomet IV. having sent a defiance to the Emperor Leopold in his christian character, threatening to ruin him, *and pursue his crucified God*, George Fox wrote a reply to this public document, warning the Turk to fear the great God that made him and all things, and showing him, out of their own Koran, that the founder of their religion wrote more respectfully of Christ; whom he then proceeds to set forth to the notice of the Sultan by citations from the Scriptures."

He also wrote as follows to the captive Friends in Algiers, warning them of an error among the Turks, and urging them to contradict it.[1]

1683.

"There is a common saying among the Turks to the christians, '*your crucified God*,' meaning Christ. Now there is a mistake in this their saying. Though God was in Christ, reconciling the world unto Himself, it *was not the eternal God, that was crucified and died*, that *was in Christ;* for Christ said, when He was about to suffer, 'My God! my God!

[1] *Journal of G. Fox.*

why hast Thou forsaken Me?' *So Christ suffered in the flesh and was crucified and died, as He was man, not as He was God — the Word which was in the beginning — but as He was man, who bore the iniquities of all mankind, and was an offering for the sins of the whole world; who tasted death for every man — all being in death in Adam — that they might have life through Christ, the second Adam.* So I say again, that Christ did not die as He was God, but as He was man. He was crucified, and buried, and arose again the third day, and ascended, and is at the right hand of God. This He did by the power of God, as He was man. So the Turks are mistaken to say, or to think, that the eternal God could be crucified or die."

The great truth that in Christ Jesus there is neither male nor female early impressed the mind of this champion for the right. He speaks in the early part of his journal of meeting with some people who contended that women had no souls, and argued against such heresy. Mention has been made of his establishment of meetings where the women might transact the affairs more particularly appertaining to their position, and he also wrote letters to this effect bringing scripture proofs to support his assertions.

One of these was addressed to the Duke of Holstein, and may be interesting in the present day.

" For the Duke of Holstein, whom I entreat, in the love of God, to read over this, which is sent in love to him.

" I understand that formerly, by some evil-minded persons, it was reported to thee, when Elizabeth Hendricks came to Frederickstadt to visit the people called Quakers, that it was a scandal to the christian religion, that a woman should be suffered to preach in a public assembly religiously gathered together. Upon which thou gave forth an order to the rulers of Frederickstadt, 'to make the said people leave that place forthwith, or to send them away.' But the said rulers being Arminians, and they, or their fathers, having come to live there, as a persecuted people in Holland, not much above three score years ago, made answer to the duke, 'They were not willing to persecute others for conscience' sake, who had looked upon persecution on that account, in their own case, as antichristian,' etc. But after that, the people of God, in scorn called Quakers, wrote unto thee, O duke, from Frederickstadt; and since that time, they have had their liberty, and their meetings peaceable, to serve and worship God almost these twenty years at Frederickstadt, and thereabouts, freely, without any molestation; which liberty they have acknowledged as a great favor and kindness from thee.

" And now, O duke, thou professing christianity from the great and mighty name of Jesus Christ, who is King of kings, and Lord of lords, and the Holy Scriptures of truth of the Old and New Testament, do not you use many women's words in your service, and worship out of the Old and New Testament? The apostle saith, 'Let your women keep silence in the churches;' and that 'he did not permit a woman to

speak, but to be under obedience, and if she will
learn anything, to ask her husband at home, for it is
a shame for a woman to speak in the church.' And
1 Tim. ii. 11, 12, ' Women are to learn in silence
and not be suffered to teach, nor to usurp authority
over the man, but to be in silence.' 1 Cor. xiv. 34.
Now, here the duke may see what sort of women
were to be in silence and in subjection, whom the
law commands to be silent, and not to usurp authority
over the man, nor to speak in the church, these were
unruly women. In the same chapter, he commands
women ' not to plait nor broider their hair, nor to
wear gold, pearls, or costly array.' These things
were forbidden by the apostle; and such women as
wear such things are to learn in silence, and to be
subject, and not to usurp authority over the men;
for it is a shame for such to speak in the church.
But do not such women as these, that wear gold and
silver, and pearls, and costly apparel, or costly array,
and plait or broider their hair, speak in your church,
when your priest sets them to sing psalms? Do not
they speak when they sing psalms? Consider this, O
duke! Yet you say, ' your women must keep silence
in the church, and must not speak in the church,'
but when they sing psalms in your churches, are
they then silent? Though the apostle forbids such
women before-mentioned to speak in the church, yet
in another place the apostle encourages the good or
holy women to be teachers of good things, as in
Titus ii. 3, 4. The apostle saith, ' I entreat thee,
true yoke-fellow, to help those women which labored
with me in the gospel, and with other my fellow-la-

borers, whose names are written in the book of life.'
Here he owns these holy women, and encourages
them, which labored with him in the gospel, and did
not forbid them. (Phil. iv. 2, 3.) He likewise commends Phœbe unto the church of the Romans, calls
her 'a servant unto the church of Cenchrea,' sends
his epistle by her to the Romans from Corinth, and
desires the church at Rome to 'receive her in the
Lord as becometh saints,' and to 'assist her in whatsoever business she had need of ; for she had been a
succorer of many, and of himself also.' And he said,
'Greet Priscilla and Aquila, my helpers in Christ
Jesus, who have for my life laid down their own
necks ; unto whom not only I give thanks, but also
all the churches of the Gentiles.' Now here the
duke may see these were good, holy women, whom
the apostle did not forbid speaking. (Rom. xvi. 1–4),
but commends them. And Priscilla and Aquila in-
structed and expounded unto Apollos the way of
God more perfectly. (Acts xviii. 26.) So here Priscilla was an instructor as well as Aquila ; which holy
women the apostle doth not forbid. Neither did the
apostle forbid Philip's four daughters, which were
virgins, to prophesy. Women might pray and prophesy in the church. (1 Cor. xi. 5.)

"The apostles showed to the Jews the fulfilling of
Joel's prophesy : 'That in the last days God would
pour out of His spirit upon all flesh, and their sons
and daughters, servants and handmaids, should prophesy with the spirit of God.' So the apostle encourages daughters and handmaids to prophesy as well as
sons ; and if they do prophesy, they must speak to

the church or people. (Joel ii. 28; Acts ii. 17, 18.) Did not Miriam the prophetess sing unto the Lord, and all the women with her, when the Lord had delivered the children of Israel from Pharaoh? Did not she praise the Lord and prophesy in the congregation of the children of Israel? and was not this in the church? (Ex. xv. 21.) Moses and Aaron did not forbid her prophesying or speaking; but Moses said, ' Would God all the Lord's people were prophets!' And the Lord's people are women as well as men. Deborah was a judge and a prophetess; and do not you make use of Deborah's and Miriam's words in your service and worship? See (Judg. v. 1-31) Deborah's large speech or song. Barak did not forbid her, nor any of the Jewish priests. Did not she make this speech or song in the congregation or church of Israel? In the book of Ruth there are good speeches of those good women, which were not forbidden. Hannah prayed in the temple before Eli, and the Lord answered her prayer. See what a speech Hannah makes, and a praising of God before Eli the high priest, who did not forbid her. (1 Sam. ii. 1-10.) Josiah the King sent his priest, with several others, to ask counsel of Huldah the prophetess, who dwelt at Jerusalem in the college. (2 Kings xxii. 14; 2 Chron. xxxiv. 22.) So here the King and his priests did not despise the counsel of this prophetess; and she prophesied to the congregation of Israel, as may be seen in these chapters.

"And in Luke i. 41-55, see what a godly speech Elizabeth made to Mary, and what a large godly speech Mary made also. Mary said, ' that the Lord did regard the low estate of His handmaid,' etc. And do not you make use in your worship and service of Mary's and Elizabeth's words from Luke i. 41–55, in your churches, and yet forbid women's speaking in your churches? Let all sorts of women speak in your churches, when they sing, and say Amen. In Luke ii., there was Anna the prophetess, a widow of about four score and four years; who departed not from the temple, but served God with fasting and prayer night and day. Did not she confess Christ Jesus in the temple, and give thanks to the Lord, and 'speak of Christ to all that looked for redemption in Jerusalem'? (Luke ii. 36–38.) So such holy women were not forbidden to speak in the church; neither in the law nor gospel. Was it not Mary Magdalene and other women that first preached Christ's resurrection to the apostles? The woman indeed (namely Eve) was first in transgression; and so they were women that first preached the resurrection of Christ Jesus; for Christ said to Mary, etc. ' Go to my brethren, and say unto them, I ascend unto my Father and to your Father, and to my God and to your God.' (John xx. 17.) And Luke xxiv. 10, it was Mary Magdalene, and Joanna, and Mary them other of James, and other women that were with them, who told the apostles, ' that Christ was risen from the dead; and their words, and these women's words, were as idle tales to the apostles, and they believed them not.' (Ibid., ver. 11.) And ver. 22, ' Certain women also of our company made us astonished,' they said; so here it may be seen, that the women's preaching the resurrection of Christ did astonish the

apostles. Christ sent these women to preach his resurrection; so it is no shame for such women to
preach Christ Jesus; neither are they to be silent
when Christ sends them. The apostle saith, 'Every
tongue shall confess to God.' (Rom. xiv. 11); and
'Every tongue shall confess that Jesus Christ is Lord,
to the glory of God the Father.' (Phil. ii. 11.) So
here it is clear that women must confess Christ as
well as men, if every tongue must confess. And the
apostle saith, 'There is neither male nor female; for
ye are all one in Christ Jesus.' (Gal. iii. 28.)

"And whereas it is said, 'Women must ask their
husbands at home,' etc., the duke knows very well
virgins have no husbands, nor widows; for Anna the
prophetess was a widow; and if Christ be the husband men must ask counsel of Him at home as well
as women, before they teach. And set the case,
that a Turk's wife should be a christian, or a Papist's
wife should be a Lutheran or a Calvinist, must they
ask or learn of their husbands at home, before they
confess Christ Jesus in the congregation of the Lord?
Their counsel will be to them to turn Turks or Papists. I entreat the duke to consider these things.
I entreat him to mind God's grace and truth in his
heart, that is come by Jesus; that by his Spirit of
grace and truth he may come to serve and worship
God in his Spirit and truth; so that he may serve
the living eternal God that made him, in his generation, and have his peace in Christ, that the world
cannot take away. And I do desire his good, peace,
and prosperity in this world, and his eternal com-

fort and happiness in the world that is everlasting.
Amen.   G. F.

" LONDON, *26th of the Eighth Month*, 1684."

Besides the foregoing, he wrote also epistles to
Friends, of one of which the following is a copy : —

" Friends and Brethren in the Lord Jesus Christ,
in whom you have all life, peace, and salvation ; walk
in Him, who is your heavenly Rock and Foundation,
that stands sure, who hath all power in heaven and
earth given unto Him.   So His power is over all.
Let your faith stand in His power, which is over all
from everlasting to everlasting, over the devil and his
power ; that in the holy, heavenly wisdom of God, ye
may be preserved and kept to God's glory, out of all
snares and temptations ; so that God's wisdom may be
justified of all His children in this day of His power,
and they all may be faithful, serving and worshiping
God in His Spirit and truth, and valiant for it upon
the earth.   For, as the apostle saith, ' They that believe are entered into their rest, and have ceased from
their own works, as God did from His.'   Now this
rest is an eternal rest in Christ, the eternal Son of
God, in whom every true believer hath everlasting
life in Christ Jesus, their rest and everlasting day.
For Christ the Rest bruiseth the serpent's head, and
through death destroyeth death and the devil, the
power of death and his works.   He is the Eternal
Rest, that giveth eternal life to His sheep.   Christ
fufilleth the prophets, and all the figures, shadows,
and ceremonies, as in the Old Testament ; and all

the promises are yea and amen in Christ, who was the Eternal Rest to all true believers in the apostles' days, and ever since, and is now. Christ is the beginning and the ending, the first and the last, who is ascended above all principalities, powers, thrones, and dominions, that He might fill all things. For 'by Jesus Christ all things were made and created, whether they be things in heaven, or things in the earth;' and He is the Eternal Rest. They that believe are entered into Christ, their Eternal Rest, in whom they have eternal life and peace with God. Wherefore, I say again, in Him who is your Rest, live and abide; for in Him ye are happy, and His blessings will rest upon you. God Almighty keep and preserve you all, His true believers, in Christ, your Rest and Peace this day. Amen. G. F.

"LONDON, *the 18th of Twelfth Month,* 1684–85."

Perceiving that the love of the world and worldly things was on the increase, George Fox says : —

" A great sense entered me of the growth and increase of pride, vanity, and excess in apparel ; and that not only amongst the people of the world, but too much also amongst some that come among us, and seemed to make profession of the truth. In the sense I had of the evil thereof, it came upon me to give forth the following, as a reproof and check thereunto : —

" The Apostle Peter saith (in 1 Pet. iii.) of the women's adorning: ' Let it not be (mark, let it not be, this is a positive prohibition) that outward adorning of plaiting the hair, and of wearing of gold, or of putting on of apparel ; but let it be the hidden man

9*

of the heart, in that which is not corruptible, even the ornament of a meek and quiet spirit, which is in the sight of God of great price ; for after this manner in the old time the holy women also, who trusted in God, adorned themselves.'

" Here ye may see what is the ornament of the holy women, which was in the sight of God of great price, and which the holy women who trusted in God adorned themselves with. But the unholy women, that trust not in God, their ornament is not a meek and a quiet spirit ; they adorn themselves with plaiting the hair, putting on of apparel, and wearing of gold ; which is forbidden by the apostle in his general epistle to the church of Christ, the true christians.

" And the apostle saith (1 Tim. ii. 9, 10), ' In like manner also that women adorn themselves in modest apparel, with shamefacedness and sobriety ; not with broidered hair, or gold, or pearls, or costly array, but (which becometh women professing godliness) with good works.'

" Here ye may see what the women were to adorn themselves with, who professed godliness ; they were not to adorn themselves with broidered hair, nor gold, nor pearls, nor costly array ; for this was not looked upon to be modest apparel for holy women, that professed godliness and good works. But this adorning or apparel is for the immodest, unshamefaced, unsober women, that profess not godliness, neither follow those good works that God commands. Therefore it doth not become men and women who profess true christianity and godliness, to be adorned with gold, or chains, or pearls, or costly array ; or with broidered hair; for these things are for the lust of the eye, the lust of the flesh, and the pride of life, which are not of the Father. All holy men and women are to mind that which is more precious than gold; who are ' redeemed not with corruptible things, as silver and gold, from your vain conversation; but with the precious blood of Christ, as of a Lamb without blemish and without spot. Therefore as obedient children to God, not fashioning yourselves according to your former lusts in your ignorance; but as He which hath called you is holy, so be ye holy in all manner of conversation.' " (1 Pet. i. 14, 15.)

It remains to be a truth that " those christians who enter most deeply into the spiritual nature of the gospel dispensation will find that it leads them into simplicity as regards their outward appearances." The new life hid with Christ in God must differ from the old life of self-indulgence, and many things will drop off like the petals of the flower, when the fruit matures. But as the outward creation differs, so peculiar temperaments differ, and there will be variety in the household of God, great variety but great unity, as the love of God and the desire to serve Him are predominant, and all things done to his glory.

" During the lifetime of George Fox there was no evidence of any disposition to enforce a uniform style of dress among Friends. They were gathered out of all classes of society, from the army, the navy, and the church; from commercial and professional circles; from the farm and the workshop, and from every religious profession in Great Britain. They embraced representatives of every rank, the rich and the poor, the high and the low, the learned and the ignorant, Cavaliers and Roundheads, Churchmen and Dissenters, and they dressed as differently as they naturally would do, under such circumstances.

" Before another generation passed away, however, that natural tendency of all human institutions, continually to gravitate earthward, unless perpetually revived and uplifted by the same Almighty Power which first gives life to them, began to manifest itself in the organization of the Society of Friends."

George Fox had several years before been "gathered to the everlasting rest and joy of his Lord," as the London Meeting testified of him ; but his noble wife, Margaret Fox, who had spent several years in various English jails, and had suffered the loss of all for Christ's sake and the gospel, entered her protest against any mere outward uniformity. In a letter written from Swarthmore, Fourth Month, 1698, she says : —

" And let us all take heed of touching anything like the ceremonies of the Jews, for that was displeasing unto Christ; for He came to bear witness against them, and testified against their outside Practices, who told them of their Long Robes and of their Broad Phylacteries, and against their Garnishing the Sepulchres of the Prophets, and told them, If the Prophets had been there, they would have killed them, as their Fathers did ; and when they found fault with him for eating and drinking with Publicans and Sinners, he told them, That Publicans and Sinners should enter into the Kingdom before them.

So that we may see how ill he liked their outward Ceremonies. So let us keep to the Rule and Leading of the Eternal Spirit, that God hath given us to be our Teacher, and let that put on and off, as is meet and serviceable for every one's State and Condition : And let us take heed of limiting in such Practices ; for we are under the Gospel Leading, and Guiding and Teaching, which is a free Spirit, which leads into Unity and Lowliness of mind the Saints and Servants of Christ, desiring to be Established in the free Spirit, not bound nor limited. Legal Ceremonies are far from Gospel Freedom ; Let us beware of being guilty, or having a hand in ordering or contriving that which is contrary to Gospel Freedom ; for the Apostle would not have Dominion over their Faith, but to be helpers of their Faith. It's a dangerous thing to lead young Friends much into the observation of outward things, which may be easily done ; for they can soon get into an outward Garb, to be all alike outwardly ; but this will not make them true christians : It's the Spirit that gives Life, I would be loth to have a hand in these things. The Lord preserve us, that we do no hurt to God's Work ; but let Him work, whose Work it is : We have lived quietly and peaceably thus far, and it's not for God's Service to make Breaches. MARGARET FOX "

CHAPTER XVI

WHILE George Fox was thus engaged in the care of the church, an event occurred which caused great changes in the English nation.

In the Second Month of 1685, the stern messenger who comes alike to palace and cottage, presented himself at Whitehall, in the midst of that corrupt court, which busied itself about anything rather than a preparation for his coming. King Charles was seized with illness, and after three days passed to the tribunal of the King of kings. His brother James, who had as Duke of York been very obnoxious to Parliament, now ascended the throne amid the acclamations of nearly all parties. He at once professed himself a Romanist, had a new pulpit erected at court for a Romish priest, and mass was publicly celebrated ·at Westminster. Still he declared that he was determined to protect the liberties of his people.

About a month after his accession to the throne a petition for relief was drawn up by the Friends, and sent to the King. They stated that above one thousand five hundred Friends, both men and women, had been detained prisoners in England and Wales. Their long and tedious imprisonment in the crowded jails had impaired the health of all, while three hundred and twenty had died in consequence. Thus many homes were made desolate, and widows and fatherless children were mourning the loss of their dear ones. Woeful havoc and spoil had also been made upon the property of those not in prison, through the fines imposed upon them. Some were left without a bed to rest upon; some with no oxen to till their fields, no corn for seed, and no tools to work with; thus preventing industry. And all this, the petition says, " under pretense of serving the King and the church, thereby to force us to a conformity, without inward conviction or satisfaction of our tender consciences, wherein our peace with God is concerned, which we are very tender of."

Action upon this petition was prevented by the attempt of the Duke of Monmouth to obtain the throne. The King and his court were fully occupied in suppressing this insurrection, and wreaking vengeance on those concerned in it. There is much to regret in the sanguine character of that vengeance; and the action of the brutal Lord Jeffries, presiding over the " bloody assize," is one of the dark stains in English history. The Duke of Argyle, who was a Presbyterian, had taken an active part in this attempt to drive James from his throne. Against this sect consequently, as well as other Dissenters, the laws were now more rigorously enforced.

A deputation of the Friends was appointed to wait upon the King, and renew their solicitations for the release of their brothers and sisters, who had been shut up in dungeons, in terms varying from five to fifteen years. While King James as a Roman Catholic had some object in desiring leniency of action toward non-conformists, it must be acknowledged that he always professed himself averse to persecution for religious belief. The deputation was favorably received, and on the 15th of Third Month, 1685, a warrant was issued, releasing the Friends who were in prison. Nearly fifteen hundred now came forth to be rejoicingly restored to their families and homes.

While so much had been gained there was need for further assistance from the King, as the laws against non-conformists were still in force, and the informers were busily at work. A statement of their perjuries and embezzlements was drawn up, and Friends petitioned to have a commission appointed to examine into its truth. The assertions were all proven and the King declared his aversion to the informers, and that it was his will they should be discountenanced.

The Yearly Meeting in the spring of 1686 was a joyful occasion. Many were present who had been for years deprived of the privilege of thus meeting with their friends, and thanksgiving and praise ascended to the Lord for their deliverance. The watchful eye of George Fox was upon these newly released prisoners, and feeling, as he says, " a concern that none might look too much to man, but might eye the Lord therein, from whom deliverance comes," he wrote the following letter : —

" FRIENDS, — The Lord, by his eternal power, hath opened the heart of the King to open the prison doors, by which about fifteen or sixteen hundred are set at liberty, and hath given a check to the informers; so that in many places our meetings are pretty quiet. My desires are, that both liberty and sufferings may be sanctified to His people, that Friends may prize the mercies of the Lord in all things, and to Him be thankful, who stilleth the raging waves of the seas, allayeth the storms and tempests, and maketh a calm. Therefore it is good to trust in the Lord, and cast your care upon Him, who careth for you. For when ye were in jails and prisons, the Lord did by His eternal arm and power uphold you, and sanctified them to you (and unto some he made them as a sanctuary), and tried His people as in a furnace of affliction, both in prisons and spoiling of goods. In all this the Lord was with His people, and taught them to know that 'the earth is the Lord's and the fullness thereof;' and that He was in all places; 'who crowneth the year with His goodness.' (Psa. lxv.) Therefore let all God's people be diligent and careful to keep the camp of God holy, pure, and clean; and to serve God and Christ and one another in the glorious, peaceable gospel of life and salvation, which glory shines over God's camp; and His great Prophet, Bishop, and Shepherd is among, or in the midst of them, exercising His heavenly offices in them; so that you, His people, may rejoice in Christ Jesus, through whom you have peace with God. For He that destroyeth the devil and his work, and bruises the serpent's head, is all God's people's heavenly Foundation and Rock to build upon, which was the holy prophets' and apostles' Rock in days past, and is now the Rock of our age; which Rock and Foundation of God standeth sure. Upon this the Lord God establish all his people. Amen. G. F.

"LONDON, *25th of the Seventh Month*, 1686."

Not only did the Friends in England receive his care, but epistles of advice and counsel were sent to the churches in the New World.

To Friends in the ministry, in Pennsylvania and New Jersey.

* "ENFIELD, *Fifth Month*, 30th, 1685.

" DEAR FRIENDS, — With my love to you all and all other Friends. I was glad to hear from you, but you gave me no account of the increase of truth among you, nor what meetings you have had amongst the Indian kings and their people, abroad in the countries, and of your visiting Friends in New England, Virginia, and Carolina, nor of your travels and labors in the gospel, though you have in all those countries, liberty to serve and worship God, and preach the truth. And I understand many have a desire to live in it especially in Carolina ; and you, who travel now to visit Friends in those provinces, it is thought strange you do not visit them (those people that were seeking the truth). . . . . And therefore my desires are, that you may all be diligent, serving the Lord and minding His glory and the prosperity of His truth this little time you have to live ; and be not like Adam, in the earth, but use this world as though you did not use it ; for they that covet after this world fall into divers snares and hurtful lusts ; and therefore consider that you are but sojourners here ; that you may pass your time in the fear of God, and you being many, and having many of the Friends of the ministry going over into those parts, you may be a hindrance one to another, if you confine your visits to Friends, and do not travel in the life of the universal truth, that would have all men to be saved and come to the knowledge of the truth ; and if *you* would have them come to a knowledge of the truth, let them know it and where it is to be found. So I desire that you be valiant for it upon the earth, that you may give a good account unto God at the last with joy. I desire that all Friends in the ministry may see this, in Pennsylvania and New Jersey. My love to you all in the holy Seed of life that reigns over all. Amen. G. F."

While George Fox so earnestly declared the blessed doctrine of the teaching of the Holy Spirit, we see by the tenor of this epistle that he fully embraced the truth that the Lord is pleased to use instrumental means in promulgating the gospel. "Let him that heareth say come," was the motive power which led him through Great Britain and America; and the blessed promise of his Master, "Lo, I am with you always," was his support and stay. Nor would he confine his ministrations to the sect of his choice ; he went himself and advised his brothers in the ministry to travel "in the life of the universal truth." Well is it for the church he loved to remember that the commission of her Master is broad, and His standing order to His followers is, "Go ye into all the world and preach the gospel to every creature." The theme of christians from the earliest formation of the church, the theme which will form the joyous strains of eternity, salvation through the blood of the Lamb, was the theme which inspired many of the epistles of George Fox. "None but Christ! none but Christ!" was his motto. See how fully this truth is brought out in a letter dated —

"KINGSTON-UPON THAMES, *Twelfth Month*, 1686.

"Christ saith, 'I am come that they might have life, and that they might have it more abundantly!' He gave His flesh for the life of the world. And He saith, 'I am the resurrection and the life;' and, 'I am the way, the truth, and the life; no man cometh unto the Father but by me.' Christ is the quickening spirit. All men being dead in Adam are to be quickened and made alive by Christ, the second Adam. And when they are quickened and made alive by Him they meet together in the name of Jesus Christ their Saviour, who died for their sins, and is risen for their justification, who was dead and is alive again, and liveth forevermore. All whom He hath quickeneth and made alive (even all the living) meet in the name of Jesus, who is alive, and He, their living Prophet, Shepherd, and Bishop, is in the midst of them; and is their living Rock and Foundation, and a living Mediator between them and the living God. So the living praise the living God through Jesus Christ, through whom they have peace with God. All the living have rest in Christ, their life. He is their sanctification, their righteousness, their treasure of wisdom, knowledge, and understanding which is spiritual and heavenly. He is the spiritual tree and root, which all the believers in the light, the life in Christ, that pass from the death in Adam to the life in Christ, and overcome the world, and are born of

God, are grafted into ; even Christ the heavenly tree, which beareth all the spiritual branches or grafts. These meet in His name, are gathered in Him, and sit together in heavenly places in Christ Jesus, their life, who hath quickened and made them alive. So all the living worship the living God in His Holy Spirit and truth, in which they live and walk. Into this worship the foul, unclean spirit, the devil, cannot get; for the Holy Spirit and truth is over him and he is out- of it. This is the standing worship, which Christ set up in His new covenant. And they that are quickened by Christ are the living stones, living members, and spiritual household and church, or congregation, of Christ, who is the living head or husband.   G. F."

The following will show his full belief that those who would realize the blessings of salvation must experience a change from the old life, a turning unto Christ.

" John the Baptist came preaching in the wilderness of Judea, saying, ' Repent ye : for the kingdom of heaven is at hand.' (Matt. iii. 2.) And when John the Baptist was cast into prison, Mark says ' That Jesus came into Galilee, preaching the gospel of the kingdom of God, and saying, The time is fulfilled, and the kingdom of God is at hand ; repent ye, and believe the gospel.' (Mark i. 14, 15.)
" Here ye may see that people must repent of their vain life and conversation, before they receive the gospel, must be turned from darkness to the light

of Christ, and from the power of Satan unto God, before they receive His Holy Spirit, and His gospel of life and salvation. The Lord commands all men everywhere to repent, and to do works meet for repentance. They must show forth that their lives and conversations are changed, and that they serve God in newness of life, with new tongues, and new hearts.   G. F.

"Gooses, *the Sixth Month*, 1687."

The corresponding fruits of the new life are clearly brought out in another short epistle, written, as he says, to show " wherein God's people should be like Him."

" God is righteous ; and He would have His people to be righteous, and to do righteously.   God is holy ; and He would have His people holy, and to do holily. God is just ; and He would have His people to be just, and to do justly to all.   God is light ; and His children must walk in His light.   God is an eternal infinite Spirit ; and His children must walk in the Spirit.   God is merciful ; and He would have His people to be merciful.   God's sun shines upon the good and the bad, and He causes the rain to fall upon the evil and the good ; so should His people do good unto all.   God is love ; and they that dwell in love, dwell in God.   Love worketh no ill to his neighbor ; therefore 'love is the fulfilling of the law.' (Rom. xiii. 10.)   The apostle says, ' All the law is fulfilled in one word, even in this, Thou shalt love thy neighbor as thyself.' (Gal. v. 14.)   ' As the Father hath loved me, so I have loved you : continue ye in my love.' (John xv. 9.) This should be the practice of all God's people.   G. F.

His own words are again : —

" And because most people would confess that God's people should be thus, but few know how to come to this state ; therefore in the openings of the spirit of truth I wrote another short paper, directing to the ' right way and means, whereby people might come unto Christ, and so be made like unto God.'

" Thus : Christ saith, ' I am the way, the truth, and the life ; no man cometh unto the Father but by me.' (John xvi. 6.) And again, ' No man can come to me, except the Father, which hath sent me, draw him.' (John vi. 44.) Now what is the means by which God doth draw people to His Son, but by His Holy Spirit, who ' poureth out of His Spirit upon all flesh.' By this Holy Spirit the holy and righteous God doth draw people from their unrighteousness and unholiness to Christ, the righteous and holy One, the great Prophet in His New Covenant and New Testament, of whom Moses, in the Old Covenant and Testament, said, God would raise up, like unto Him, and whom people should ' hear in all things ; and they who would not hear Him should be cut off.' They that do not hear the Son of God, the great Prophet, do not mind the drawing of the Father by His Holy Spirit to His Son ; but to them that mind the drawings of the good Spirit of the Father to His Son the Spirit giveth understanding to know God and Jesus Christ, which is eternal life. Then they know that Jesus Christ is the way, the truth, and the life, and that none can come unto God but by and through His Son, who is their Shepherd to feed them in His pastures and springs of life; and His sheep know His holy voice, in whom there was no sin, and in whose mouth there was no guile; and an hireling they will not hear, for he careth not for the sheep; for they are not the hireling's, but Christ's, who hath laid down His life for His sheep. He that robs and steals his neighbor's words, that climbeth up another way, and entereth not by the door, is a thief and a robber; but Christ is the door into His sheepfold, for His sheep to enter in by. They know that Christ is the Bishop of their souls, to see that they do not go astray from God, nor out of His pastures of life; they know that Christ is their Mediator, and makes their peace with God; and they know that Christ is their High Priest, made higher than the heavens, and hath died for their sins, doth cleanse them with His blood, is risen for their justification; and is able to the utmost to save all that come to God by Him.   G. F.

"Gooses, *the Sixth Month*, 1687."

In the Fourth Month, 1687, the King issued an order that the execution of all penal laws concerning ecclesiastical matters should be suspended. This would have been more acceptable had it been the action of the King and his Parliament, rather than merely the exercise of his royal prerogative; but the liberty was enjoyed, and, in common with other Dissenters, Friends presented an address to King James expressing their thankfulness. This was favorably received, and at the assembling of the Yearly Meeting in 1687 it was concluded to send an address from that body to 'the King by the hands of William Penn, who had free access to the royal person. To this address the King returned the following answer : —

"GENTLEMEN, — I thank you heartily for your address. Some of you know, I am sure you do, Mr. Penn, that it was always my principle that conscience ought not to be forced, and that all men ought to have the liberty of their conscience. And what I have promised in my declaration I will continue to perform as long as I live ; and I hope, before I die, to settle it so that after ages shall have no reason to alter it."

King James was not to be the instrument of establishing liberty of conscience in England. His power was already tottering, and further steps in this direction caused a great excitement in his Parliament. The English people feared that toleration with him only meant favor to the Roman Catholic religion ; and the appointment of those who professed that faith to the highest offices in the state increased the feeling of anxiety. Attention was directed towards the Prince and Princess of Orange, as the hope of the nation at this crisis. The Prince, it will be remembered, was a grandson of Charles I., and his wife a daughter of James II. She had been educated in the

Protestant religion by the express orders of Charles II., and their marriage had been arranged by King James to satisfy the growing discontent of his subjects. Mary, the Princess of Orange, was the heir apparent of the crown of England, and it was to her and her husband that the eyes of the English nation were turned in this emergency.

It does not come within the scope of this work to detail the events which placed them upon the throne. It is sufficient to say that James, becoming alarmed for his personal safety, fled to France, and William and Mary were crowned King and Queen of England, in the Fourth Month, 1689.

CHAPTER XVII

A PROTESTANT King and Queen being now seated on the throne of England, with a Parliament united with them in the policy of maintaining that form of religion, the first subject claiming their attention was the modification of the laws in relation to Dissenters. An Act of Toleration was prepared " which exempted Protestant subjects, dissenting from the Church of England, from the penalties of certain laws, designed to force them to conformity."

Friends were on the alert to have the act framed so as to include them within its scope. This was very necessary, as the bill had a confession of faith attached to it, which had been drawn up with the idea of exempting the " Quakers " from its provisions, on the plea that they were not christians.

It was not to be expected that our aged veteran, who had so long counseled his brethren, would keep aloof from this conflict. In his journal he says : " Though I was weak in body, and not well able to stir about, yet so great a concern was upon my spirit on behalf of truth and Friends, that I attended continually with many Friends at the Parliament House, laboring with the members that the thing might be done comprehensively and effectually."

A confession of faith was drawn up by Friends and presented to Parliament by a committee of their body, who were examined in relation to it. The result of the investigation was that Parliament was convinced that Quakerism was not adverse to christianity.

Their profession of faith may be interesting to the Friends of the present day.

. *Question.* Do you believe the divinity and humanity of Jesus Christ, the Eternal Son of God? or that Jesus Christ is truly God and man?

Answer. Yes, we verily believe that Jesus Christ is truly God and man, according as Holy Scriptures testify of Him; God over all blessed forever; the true God, and eternal life; the one Mediator between God and man, even the man Christ Jesus.

Question. Do you believe and expect salvation and justification by the righteousness and merits of Jesus Christ, or by your own righteousness and works?

Answer. By Jesus Christ, His righteousness, merits, and works, and not by our own. God is not indebted to us for our deservings, but we to Him for His free grace in Christ Jesus; whereby we are saved through faith in Him, not of ourselves; and by His grace are enabled truly and acceptably to serve and follow Him as He requires. He is our all in all, who worketh all in us that is well pleasing to God.

Question. Do you believe in the remission of sins and redemption through the sufferings, death, and blood of Christ?

Answer. Yes, through faith in Him, as He suffered and died for all men, gave Himself a ransom for all, and His blood being shed for the remission of sins, so all they who sincerely believe in and obey Him receive the blessed effects of His suffering and dying for them. They, by faith in His name, receive and partake of that eternal redemption which He hath obtained for us, who gave Himself for us that He might redeem us from all iniquity. He died for our sins, and rose again for our justification, and " if we walk in the light, as He is in the light, we have fellowship one with another, and the blood of Jesus Christ, His Son, cleanseth us from all sin."

And now the long-looked-for relief had come, and Friends in common with other Dissenters were relieved in some measure from the suffering which had pressed so heavily upon them. They could meet in peace to worship God, and were no longer required to take an oath. Tithes were still demanded, and they suffered the loss of property in that respect, but the cruel imprisonments ceased.

No one rejoiced more in this deliverance than George Fox, whose body was now feeling the effects of his earnest labor for his Master, but whose spirit was fresh and strong. Like the beloved disciple of old, love was the prevailing feeling in his heart, and love the burden of his exhortations to the people.

Writing from London under date Third Month, 23d, 1689, he says : —

" Dear Friends and Brethren in Christ Jesus, whom the Lord by His eternal arm and power hath preserved to this day, all walk in the power and Spirit of God, that is over all, in love and unity ; for love overcomes, builds up, and unites all the members of Christ to Him the Head. Love keeps out of all strife and is of God. Love as charity never fails, but keeps the mind above all outward things and strife about all outward things. It overcomes evil, and casts out all false fears. It is of God, and unites all the hearts of His people in the heavenly joy, concord, and unity. The God of love preserve you all, and establish you in Christ Jesus, your life and salvation, in whom ye have all peace with God. So walk in Him, that ye may be ordered in His peaceable heavenly wisdom, to the glory of God and the comfort one of another."

The pressure of care devolving upon George Fox in London was so great that his bodily strength was not sufficient for long visits to the city. His step-sons-in-law had pleasant country homes near London, and in one or the other of these he found rest for his enfeebled frame. A warm affection seems to have existed between him and the members of his wife's family, and he was always warmly welcomed in their homes. In a written testimonial to his memory they say that " they found him a tender father, who never failed to give them wholesome counsel, and that the esteem they entertained for him in early life was increased by a longer and more intimate acquaintance."

Margaret Fox came from her home at the North and spent the winter of 1689 with him, but her family and estate requiring her care, she returned to Swarthmore in the spring. The single-hearted devotion with which these two endeavored to serve their Master will be seen from Margaret Fox's own words. " Though the Lord had provided an outward habitation for him, yet he was not willing to stay at it, because it was so remote and far from London, where his work lay. And my concern for God and for His holy eternal truth was then in the North, where God had placed and sent me, and likewise for the ordering and governing of my children and family, so that we were very willing both of us to live apart some years upon God's account, and His truth's service, and to deny ourselves of that comfort which we might have had in being together, for the sake and service of the Lord and His truth."

As the organization of the Society had now been satisfactorily established, it is probable that he had an idea of retiring to Swarthmore in the winter of 1690, to obtain the repose his declining years required. Before that time, however, his Master called him to "come up higher," to the "house not made with hands, eternal in the heavens." It is obvious to any one who has followed the life of this earnest laborer that he had neither time nor inclination for the accumulation of wealth. He seems to have been in the possession of enough to gratify his own simple wants, and in some measure to provide for others. With this he was content, and so far from seeking to be rich, he even refused it when circumstances placed it in his power, as we have seen when he refused any part or lot in his wife's inheritance.

Some time before this he had purchased a piece of land in the neighborhood of Swarthmore, and one of the later acts of his life was to give this to Friends, as a site for a meeting-house. The terms of the grant are as follows: " I offer and give up freely to the Lord, for the service of His sons and daughters and servants, called Quakers, the house and houses, barn and kiln, stable and all the land, with the garden and orchard, being about three acres of land, more or less, with all the commonage, great turfing, moss, with whatever privileges belonging to it, called Pettis at Swarthmore, in the parish of Ulverstone. And also my ebony bedstead with painted curtains, and the great elbow chair that Robert Widders sent me, and my great sea-case with the bottles in it, I do give to stand in the house as heirlooms, when the house shall be made use of as a meeting-place, so that Friends (who go to lodge there) may have a bed to lie on, a chair to sit on, and a bottle to hold a little water to drink." After mentioning the repairs and the necessity of making a road-way, etc., he continues, "You may let any poor honest Friend live in the house, and so let it all be for the Lord's service to the end of the world."

Swarthmore meeting-house, thus built and endowed by George Fox, is still standing, and "the great elbow chair" is still there, and some pieces of the "ebony bedstead." And there, too, may be seen the Bible with the chain by which it was formerly fastened to the minister's gallery.

The shades of evening were now fast gathering about this useful life, but the busy pen was still in motion, as with keen-sighted watchfulness error was detected in the ranks of the loved Society.

In the Second Month of 1690 he says: "I had a concern upon my spirit with respect to a twofold danger that attended some who professed truth: one was of young people's running into the fashions of the world ; and the other was of old people's going into earthly things." He accordingly wrote this letter : —

" To all who profess the Truth of God, — My desires are that you may walk in humility in it. For when the Lord first called me forth, he let me see that young people grew up together in vanity, and the fashions of the world; and old people went downward into the earth, raking it together. And now, Friends, I see too many young people, that profess the truth, grow up into the fashions of the world, and too many parents indulge them; and amongst the elder some are going downwards and raking after the earth. Therefore take heed that you are not making your graves, while you are alive outwardly, and loading yourselves with thick clay. (Hab. xi. 6.) For if you have not power over the worldly spirit, and that which leadeth into a vain mind, and the fashions of the world and into the earth; though you have often had the rain fall upon your fields, you will but bring forth thistles, briers, and thorns, which are for the fire. Such will become brittle, peevish, fretful spirits, that will not abide the heavenly doctrine, the admonitions, exhortations, and reproofs of the Holy Ghost, or Heavenly Spirit of God, which would bring you to be conformable to the death of Christ, and to His image, that ye might have fellowship with Him in His resurrection. Therefore it is good for all to bow to the name of Jesus their Saviour, that all may confess Him to the glory of God. For I have a concern upon me, in a sense of the danger of young people's going into

10*

earthly things, and many going into a loose and false
liberty, till at last they go quite out into the spirit
of the world, as some have done. The house of such
hath been built upon the sand by the sea-shore, not
upon Christ, the Rock; that they are so soon in the
world again, under a pretense of liberty of conscience. But it is not a pure conscience, nor in the
Spirit of God nor in Christ Jesus; for in the liberty
of the Spirit there is the unity which is the bond of
peace, and all are one in Christ Jesus, in whom is
the true liberty; and this is not of the world, for He
is not of the world. Therefore all are to stand fast
in Him, as they have received Him, for in Him there
is peace, who is the Prince of Peace; but in the world
there is trouble. For the spirit of the world is a
troublesome spirit, but the Spirit of Christ is a peaceable Spirit; in which God Almighty preserve all the
faithful. Amen."

The following advice to ministers of the gospel is
applicable at the present day, though nearly two
hundred years have elapsed since it was written: —

" All Friends in the ministry everywhere, to whom
God hath given a gift of the ministry, and who travel
up and down in it, do not hide your talent, nor put
your light under a bushel, nor cumber or entangle
yourselves with the affairs of this world. For the
natural soldiers are not to cumber themselves with
the world, much less the soldiers of Christ, who are
not of this world, but are to mind the riches and
glory of the world that is everlasting. Therefore

stir up the gift of God in you and improve it ; do not sit down Demas-like, and embrace this present world that will have an end, lest ye become idolaters. Be valiant for God's truth upon the earth, and spread it abroad in the daylight of Christ, you who have sought the kingdom of God and the righteousness thereof, and have received it and preached it ; which stands in 'righteousness and peace and joy in the Holy Ghost.' As able ministers of the Spirit, sow to the Spirit, that of the Spirit ye may reap life everlasting. Go on in the Spirit, plowing with it in the purifying hope ; and thrashing with the power and Spirit of God the wheat out of the chaff of corruption, in the same hope. For he that looks back from the spiritual plow into the world is not fit for the spiritual and everlasting kingdom of God, and is not like to press into it as the faithful do. Therefore, you that are awakened to righteousness, and to a knowledge of the truth, keep yourselves awakened in it ; then the enemy cannot sow his tares in your fields ; for truth and righteousness are over him and before he was. My desires are, that all may fulfill their ministry that the Lord Jesus hath committed to them ; and then, by the blood and testimony of Jesus, you will overcome the enemy that opposes it, within and without. All you that preach the truth, do it as it is in Jesus, in love ; and to all that are believers in Jesus and receivers of Him, He gives power to become the sons of God, and joint heirs of Christ, whom He calls brethren ; and He gives them the water of life, which shall be as a well in them springing up as a river to eternal life, that they may water the

spiritual plants of the living God: So that all may
be spiritual planters and spiritual waterers, and may
see with the spiritual eye the everlasting, eternal
God over all, to give the increase, who is the infinite
fountain. My desires are that you may be kept out
of the beggarly elements of the world, which are
below the spiritual region, to Christ, the Head; and
may hold Him who bruiseth the head of enmity, and
was before it was; that ye may all be united together
in love in your Head, Christ, and be ordered by His
heavenly, gentle, peaceable wisdom, to the glory of
God. For all that be in Christ are in love, peace,
and unity. In Him they are strong, and in a full
persuasion; and in Him who is the first and the
last they are in a heavenly resolution and confidence
for God's everlasting honor and glory. Amen.

" From him who is translated into the kingdom of
his dear Son, with all his saints, a heavenly saluta-
tion. Salute one another with the holy kiss of
charity, that never faileth.   G. F.

"Ford Green, *the 25th of Ninth Month,* 1690."

It is interesting to see the assurance of faith evinced
in the writings and teachings of this evangelist.
From the day when in his distress he heard the
words, " There is one, even Christ Jesus, who can
speak to thy condition," until the close of his life,
his faith never wavered. He knew that he had become a new man in Christ Jesus, and never hesitated
to declare his position as a redeemed and accepted
child of God through the atonement and mediation
of his Lord and Saviour. He could say with the

beloved disciple, " We may know Him that is true, and we are in Him that is true, even in his Son Jesus Christ. This is the true God and eternal life." But, while thus bold in asserting his position, his soul, like the Psalmist, made her boast in the Lord, and he was ever careful to declare that it was all of Christ. " We are nothing ; Christ is all."

And while resting all his hopes of pardon on a crucified Saviour he also magnified the power of a risen Lord in keeping from sin. In a general epistle to Friends written in 1662, we find very clear teaching on this doctrine of deliverance from the power of sin, the blessedness of a present Saviour, " able to save to the uttermost those who come unto God by Him."

He says : " The teachers of this world who called themselves the ministers of Christ told us that they had received a gift from Christ, who did ascend on high, and led captivity captive ; and this gift was for the work of the ministry, and for the perfecting of the saints ; and how that they were to bring people to the knowledge of the Son of God, from whence they had received this gift, and to the unity of the faith ; which faith gives the victory, and brings to have access to God, and also to a perfect man's state, and to the measure of the stature of the fullness of Christ. And thus people followed them, and were glad that they would bring them to a perfect man's state, that is, to the state of Adam and Eve before they fell, for they were perfect then ; and when we had followed them, some twenty, some thirty, some more, some less years, then they told us again, that

they hoped we would not look for perfection while
we were upon the earth, on this side the grave, for
we must carry a body of sin about us; and they
hoped we would not look for perfection, and would
not hold the erroneous doctrine of perfection. . . . .
Now of what value and price and worth have they
made the blood of Christ, that cleanseth from sin and
death; and yet told people that they would bring
them to the knowledge of the Son of God, and to a
perfect man, and now tell them they must not be perfect on the earth, but carry a body of sin about them
to the grave? As much as to say, they must be in
the state of their father Adam and their mother Eve
in the fall, under the wrath, curse, and woe, and must
not come to the state they were in before they fell, to
the image of God, in righteousness and true holiness.
And yet, ask them for what end Christ came — they
will say to destroy the devil and his works. And
then ask them if the body of sin and death be not
the devil's works and imperfection — they will say,
yes; and so are in confusion. Christ came to destroy
the devil and his works, they say, and yet they must
carry them to the grave; and yet people are saved by
Christ, they will say; but while you are upon earth,
you must not be made free from sin.

" This is as much as if one should be in Turkey a
slave, chained to a boat, and one should come to redeem him to go into his own country; but, say the
Turks, Thou art redeemed, but while thou art upon
the earth thou must not go out of Turkey, nor have
the chain off thee. So it is said, You are redeemed,
but must carry a body of death about you, and can-

not go to your father Adam's house before he fell, but
you must live in your father Adam's house in the fall,
while ye be upon earth. But, I say, you are redeemed
by Christ; it cost Him His blood to purchase man out
of this state he is in, in the fall, and bring him up to
the state man was in before he fell : so Christ became
a curse, to bring man out of the curse ; and bore the
wrath, to bring man to the peace of God that he
might come to the blessed state, and to Adam's state
which he was in before he fell ; and not only thither,
but to a state in Christ that shall never fall. And
this is my testimony to you and to all people on the
earth. Now mark, the apostle said, *He hath quickened us, who were dead in sins and trespasses, and
hath made us to sit together in the heavenly places in
Christ Jesus ; that in the ages to come He might show
forth his exceeding riches and kindness towards us.*
Now the ages are come, glory to the Lord God over
all, in the highest forever, that this kindness and this
riches are seen, that the apostle's preaching is fulfilled, who said, *He hath quickened us, and made us
sit together in the heavenly places in Christ Jesus.* So
mark, in Christ Jesus, [*us*] the church, [*us*] the
saints, [*us*] the believers and true christians, made
us to sit together. Here was their meeting, here was
their sitting in the heavenly places in Christ Jesus,
the second Adam, the Lord from heaven; Him that
was glorified with the Father before the world began;
Him that never fell, but fetched man and woman out
of the fall, to the state that man and woman were in
before they fell ; and to sit in heavenly places in
Christ Jesus. And there is the safe sitting, in Christ

the new and living way, the word of God, the power
of God, the Light, the Life and Truth, in the First
and in the Last, in the Beginning and in the Ending,
in Him in whom there is no shadow of turnings nor
variableness. G. F."

The Friends in Ireland were passing through great
suffering. Many were immured in prison, and others
lost all their property. The loss sustained by Friends
in 1689 was estimated at £100,000. George Fox
deeply felt their condition, and the last letter he
wrote was to encourage and cheer them. It is as
follows : —

" Dear Friends and Brethren in the Lord Jesus
Christ, whom the Lord by His eternal arm and power
hath upheld through your great sufferings, exercises,
trials, and hardships, up and down that nation, which
I am very sensible of ; and the rest of the faithful
Friends who have been partakers with you in your
sufferings, and who cannot but suffer with the Lord's
people that suffer. My confidence hath been in the
Lord, that He would and will support you in all your
sufferings ; and that He would preserve all the faithful in His wisdom, that they might give no just occasion to one nor other to make them suffer ; and, if
you did suffer wrongfully or unjustly, that the righteous God would assist and uphold you, and reward
them according to their works that oppressed or
wronged you. And now my desire is unto the Lord
that in the same holy and heavenly wisdom ye may
all be preserved to the end of your days, to the glory

of God, minding His supporting hand and power who
is God, all sufficient to strengthen, help, and refresh
in time of need.   Let none forget the Lord's mercies
and kindnesses, which endure forever, but always
live in the sense of them.   And truly, Friends, when
I consider the thing, it is the great mercy of God
that ye have not been all swallowed up, seeing with
what spirits ye have been compassed about.   But the
Lord carries his lambs in His arms, and they are as
tender to Him as the apple of His eye, and His power
is His hedge about His vineyard of heavenly plants·
Therefore it is good for all His children to be given
up to the Lord, with their minds and souls, hearts
and spirits, who is a faithful Keeper, that neither
slumbers nor sleeps, but is able to preserve and keep
you and to save to the utmost ; and none can hurt so
much as a hair of your heads, except He suffer it to
try you ; for He upholds all things in heaven and in
earth by the Word of His power.   All things were
made by Christ, and by Him all things consist,
whether they be visible or invisible.   So He hath
power over all, for all power in heaven and in earth
is given to Him ; and to you that have received Him
He hath given power to become the sons and daughters of God ; so living members of Christ, the living
Head, grafted into Him in whom ye have eternal
life.   Christ the Seed reigns, and His power is over
all ; who bruises the serpent's head, and destroys the
devil and his works, and was before he was.   So all
of you live and walk in Christ Jesus, that nothing
may be between you and God, but Christ in whom
ye have salvation."

It must have been a great comfort to George Fox
to be able to use the closing words of this epistle:
" I hear that in Germany and Holland, and there-
away, Friends are in love, unity, and peace ; and in
Jamaica, Barbadoes, Nevis, Antigua, Maryland, and
New England, I hear nothing but Friends are in
unity and peace." His life had been one of outward
turmoil and disturbance ; but now at eventide the
clouds dispersed, and the setting sun shone out with
a peaceful radiance.

The day after he had written this letter being
First Day, he attended the meeting in Gracechurch
Street, and was enabled to preach with great power
and clearness. His voice was afterwards heard in
prayer, commending himself and his friends to the
loving care of his Lord and Saviour. Going to a
Friend's house to dinner, he complained of not feeling
well, saying, " I felt the cold strike to my heart as I
came out of meeting ; " but added, " I am glad I was
there ; now I am clear, now I am fully clear." He
was obliged to lie down, and it was soon apparent
that his strength was failing. But he still maintained his care for the promotion of the cause of the
Lord, and counseled with his friends about circulating books which would teach the doctrines he loved.
To those who came to see him he said, " All is well :
the Seed of God reigns over all and over death itself."
And he says, " Though I am weak in body, yet the
power of God is over all, and the Seed reigns over
all disorderly spirits." Shortly before his death,
being asked how he found himself, he replied, " Never
heed : the Lord's power is over all weakness and

death." Thus calmly he passed through the valley of the shadow of death, and even as his feet touched the river he sent back a triumphant cry, " The Seed reigns, blessed be the Lord." The Lord Jesus whom he loved, of whom he so often spoke as the blessed Seed of God, was with His servant; and, being made conqueror through faith in the all-atoning blood of Jesus, he entered into rest, Eleventh Month 13th, 1690, in the sixty-seventh year of his age. On' the day of his burial, a very large company gathered in the meeting-house at White-Hart Court to pay the last tribute of respect to his memory. There were many loving testimonies borne to the effect of his ministry and his earnest labor for the welfare of the Society of Friends, while the honor and glory were ascribed unto the Lord, who had called and qualified him for His service. After the meeting, his body, in a plain, simple coffin, was carried on the shoulders of some of the Friends to its grave in Bunhill-Fields, followed by thousands of Friends, in long procession, three abreast, and there he was laid to rest.

He had been toiling all the night long, but now the day had dawned, — the bright, glorious day which hath no ending.

> " Oh, he was unto glory borne!
> On the deep trouble-sea
> Tossed fearfully;
> Now by Christ's blood,
> A stronger flood,
> He is at rest where he would be.

"No more, no more his soul shall faint
  With the day's heat and care :
  Storms reach not there.
  His life-work done,
  His life-race run,
Only a weight of joy to bear."

" *He being dead yet speaketh.*"

Lightning Source UK Ltd.
Milton Keynes UK
UKHW022044230219
337879UK00010B/1055/P